SUGGESTIONS TO TEACHERS AND STUDENTS

The study will be of far less value if you use the answer key during your study. A good suggestion would be to not use the key until you have completed the course, then check your answers against the answer key beginning on page 95.

PUZZLE WITH THREE PIECES

Printed by Grace Life Publishing, Inc 2001.

TABLE OF CONTENTS*

*Regular type numbers refer to text. Italicized numbers refer to same chapter in ANSWER KEY.

INTRODUCTION

THE STUDY OF GENESIS THROUGH REVELATION

As you begin your adventure of studying through the Bible, be prepared for the joy and awe you will experience when you see the completed picture of God's working with mankind. Have you ever put together a large puzzle with hundreds of pieces? You gathered similar colors and designs and put those pieces together. Slowly, those similar clustered pieces were joined together and little by little you finished the puzzle. Remember the feeling of satisfaction you experienced as you were able to see the completed picture? Your study through the Bible will be the same. As you read the questions and answer them, the Bible will slowly begin to unfold. The study will not only reveal the progression of history but as various verses are clustered together, subjects of the Bible will also be explored. These clustered subjects fit together in the overall picture, and little by little they are joined until the majestic picture of the Bible is revealed. Imagine how you will feel as you gaze on the completed picture.

OUTLINE OF THE BIBLE

In order to understand the Bible LITERALLY, it is necessary to know the three groups of people who are addressed in the Bible: the Gentiles, the Jews, and the Church, the Body of Christ. Read: 1 Corinthians 10:32.

- Genesis 1-11: God deals with GENTILES, people who are not Jews.
- Genesis 12 through mid-Acts, the nation of ISRAEL, the Jews.
- Mid-Acts through Philemon, the CHURCH, THE BODY OF CHRIST.
- Hebrews through Revelation, ISRAEL.

Look at the chart in the back of the book. Locate these groups of people. Look at the bottom of the chart and locate the books of the Bible. Which books tell about the Gentiles? Israel? The Church, Christ's Body?

HOW THE BIBLE CAME TO US

The Bible in its original writings is VERBALLY INSPIRED by God and is complete in matters of faith and practice. Second Timothy 3:16, "All scripture is inspired by God and is profitable for teaching, for reproof, for correction, for training in righteousness." The Greek word for inspired is "theopneustos" which means "God breathed." The Scriptures came into being by the breath of God. Second Peter 1:21 says, "For no prophecy was ever made by an act of human will, but men moved by the Holy Spirit spoke from God."

WRITERS OF THE BIBLE

God used godly men to write the Bible. These men had different vocations such as David, who was a shepherd/king; Luke, a doctor; Paul a Jewish leader/tentmaker, Peter; a fisherman; Moses, an Egyptian ruler/shepherd; and Hosea, a farmer.

LANGUAGES USED TO WRITE THE BIBLE

The three languages that were used to write the Bible were Hebrew, Aramaic and Greek. Hebrew and Aramaic were the languages of trade and commerce and were used to write the Old Testament. The New Testament was written in Greek. The original writings had no chapters and verses. Chapters and verses were ascribed to Archbishop Stephen Langston of Canterbury in 1227 A.D. and Cardinal Hugo de St. Caro in 1248 A.D.

THE BIBLE IS THE INERRANT WORD OF GOD

The Bible is characterized by total internal agreement or harmony. It took 40 men a period of 1,600 years to produce the 66 books of the Bible. The original writings of these inspired authors are the inerrant Word of God. The majority of these men never knew each other. They lived during different time periods and in different locations. Each book is a complete account and yet it is only a part of an ongoing history. Remarkably, all of the 40 writers AGREE.

THE BIBLE SAYS IT IS THE WORD OF GOD

By using terms such as "thus saith the Lord," or "the Lord spoke," or "the Word of the Lord came to," or the commandments of the Lord the Bible writers declared some 3,800 times that the Bible is the Word of God. Jesus Christ confirmed that the Law and the Prophets were scripture and could not be broken (John 10:34-35).

THE BIBLE IS NOT A SCIENCE OR HISTORY BOOK, BUT WHEN IT DEALS WITH THESE SUBJECTS, IT IS 100% ACCURATE.

PROPHECY PROVES THE INFALLIBILITY OF THE BIBLE

Prophecy is something that God says will happen and it is fulfilled 100% of the time. The Bible gives well over 1,000 prophecies about cities, nations, earth, man, angels, and over 300 prophecies concerning Jesus Christ. There are prophecies that tell of Christ's miraculous ministry, crucifixion, burial, resurrection, and ascension, His coming Kingdom, and other aspects of His ministry. Many of these prophecies have already been fulfilled but others remain yet to be fulfilled. As surely as God has accomplished the majority of these prophecies, the rest also will be fulfilled.

HOW TO STUDY THE BIBLE

The Bible is to be taken literally. As you read the Bible, it is important to ask yourself the questions:

> WHO is being spoken of?
> WHAT is being said?
> WHEN is it being said?
> WHERE was it said?
> WHY was it said?

WHAT IS THE INDUCTIVE BIBLE STUDY METHOD?

The inductive Bible study method is a method where you, without human guidance, can study through the Bible. As you look up the verses in the Bible, those Bible facts will answer the questions. Slowly, as bits and pieces of Bible facts are gathered, you will discover Bible concepts in God's progressive working with mankind from Genesis through Revelation. Gradually, you will be able to articulate that Bible knowledge. The Bible recognizes this method of study as the "line upon line, precept upon precept" method.

BE PREPARED TO BE CHANGED

As you answer the WHO? WHAT? WHEN? WHERE? and WHY? questions, you will begin to have an understanding of the Bible literally from Genesis through Revelation. The Bible will bring you face to face with the Lord Jesus Christ and as you behold His glory, YOU WILL BE CHANGED. Second Corinthians 3:18 says, "But we all, with unveiled face beholding as in a mirror the glory of the Lord, are being transformed into the same image from glory to glory." Are you ready to be more like the Lord Jesus?

CHAPTER 1

GOD CREATED THE HEAVENS AND THE EARTH

What a way to begin! The focus is on God, His power, and His creation. The word "Genesis" means beginnings and in Genesis you will read of the beginning of the universe, heaven, sin, redemption, the earth, nations, languages, nation of Israel, manufacturing, cattle raising, etc. Genesis covers a period of about 2,000 years. From the account of God creating the heavens and earth in Genesis 1 until the creation of the New Heaven and New Earth in Revelation 21, there is a period of about 7,000 years. This is the history of mankind.

Your adventure through the Bible begins at the:

ORIGINAL CREATION

Read: Genesis 1:1. What did God create?

Read: Genesis 1:2. What was "dark and void?"

Did God create the heavens and earth "dark and void?" Isaiah 45:18. Some Bible teachers believe the word "was" should be translated "became". Then it would read: "And the earth became dark and void."

Does the Bible tell of any possible cause of this dark chaotic time? It is possible that the original creation became "dark and void" when Satan and his angels were cast to the earth.

HOW SIN ENTERED THE UNIVERSE

Read: Ezekiel 28:12-18 and Isaiah 14:12-14. God created the angels.
Who was the anointed cherub? Isaiah 14:12

"Helel" in the Hebrew could be translated "Lucifer" or "the shining one."

Describe the anointed cherub. Ezekiel 28:12-15; Isaiah 14:13-14
a._____ b._____ c._____ d._____ e._____

What job did the anointed cherub have? Ezekiel 28:14

How did Lucifer sin? Isaiah 14:13-14; Ezekiel 28:15-17
a._____ b._____ c._____

Where was Lucifer cast after he sinned? Ezekiel 28:17

Who else was thrown to earth? Revelation 12:9

Lucifer's name was changed to what? Revelation 12:9
a._____ b._____ c._____ d._____

1

What did the fallen angels become? Luke 4:33-36

Where did Satan later appear? Ezekiel 28:13

Who observed Satan falling from heaven? Luke 10:18

How does Satan appear today? 2 Corinthians 11:13-14

What is another name for Satan? Revelation 9:11
"Abaddon" could be translated "Destroyer."

What did Satan destroy? Genesis 1:2

RESTORATION OF THE EARTH

How did God judge this chaotic time? 2 Peter 3:5-6

How did God prepare the earth for the habitation of man? Psalm 104:30

NOTE:

The conflict of the ages, between God and Satan, had begun! As you study through Genesis, notice the pattern that repeatedly occurs, God works, Satan destroys, then God restores.

On the first day, what did God create? Genesis 1:3-5

On the second day, what did God create? Genesis 1:6-8

On the third day, what did God create? Genesis 1:9-13

On the fourth day, what did God create? Genesis 1:14-19

On the fifth day, what did God create? Genesis 1:20-23

On the sixth day, what did God create? Genesis 1:24-31

On the seventh day, what did God do? Genesis 2:1-3

How long were the creative days? Genesis 1:8,13,19

How did God create the universe and the earth? Hebrews 11:3

2

THE ATTRIBUTES OF GOD

What is your mental image of God? What do you think He is like? Describe Him. Too often God is erroneously seen as a policeman, ready to punish; or a white-headed passive granny, who condones everything people do; or a bellhop, ready to provide a service. Are you ready to discover what God is really like from the Scriptures? Look up the verses. Read them out loud. Think of what the verses are saying about God.

God is _____. Read: John 4:24

God is _____. He is so big He cannot be measured. 1 Kings 8:27; Jeremiah 23:24

God is _____. He has no beginning and He will never end. Psalm 90:2

God is _____. What does that mean? 1 Chronicles 29:11; Daniel 4:35

God is _____. Isaiah 46:10; Psalm 147:5

How powerful is God? Job 42:2

God does not _____. Malachi 3:6

God is _____. Psalm 106:1

God is _____. Meaning He is sinless and pure. Psalm 99:9

God is _____. 1 John 4:8

God is _____. What He says will happen. John 17:17

God is _____. He judges in holiness. Jeremiah 12:1

God is _____. His way is best. Daniel 2:20

God is _____. He always keeps His word. 2 Thessalonians 3:3

God is _____. He is great and mighty. Psalm 104:1

God is _____. He is compassionate and holds back punishment. James 5:11

LIFE APPLICATION

The Person of God is the most crucial teaching in the Bible because what people know about God determines how they will live their lives. Think about it for a moment. How will knowing that God is all-powerful help you today? What changes will it make in your life by knowing that God is all-knowing? All-powerful? Sovereign? Let's look at another attribute of God.

GOD, A TRINITY

Read: Genesis 1:1. The word "God" in the Hebrew is "Elohim" and could be translated "a plural one."

Who are the three persons of God? 1 Thessalonians 1:3-5
a._____ b._____ c._____

There is one God, in three persons. This is called the Trinity.

Did you know that man also is a trinity?

MAN, A TRINITY

How did God make man? Genesis 1:26

What did God breathe into Adam? Genesis 2:7

Name the three parts of man. 1 Thessalonians 5:23
a._____ b._____ c._____

The Hebrew word "life" could be translated "lives." God breathed into Adam the breath of lives. Just as God is a plural one, a trinity, so also is man a plural one, a trinity.

LIFE APPLICATION

Did you know that God not only made you a trinity but that He gave you eternal life? Our physical bodies will die but our soul and spirit (the real us) will live forever--in Heaven with God. Those who do not trust in Christ as their Savior will live separated from God forever. John 3:16

How was Eve made? Genesis 2:21-23

Where did Adam and Eve live? Genesis 2:15

The word "Eden" means delight. The garden must have been beautiful.
What did God want Adam and Eve to do? Genesis 1:26

HOW SIN ENTERED THE HUMAN RACE

GOD'S COMMANDS

What command did God give to Adam and Eve? Genesis 2:17

What other commands did God give Adam? Genesis 1:28; 2:15
a._____ b._____

What did God tell Adam to eat? Genesis 1:29-30

What punishment would be applied for disobeying? Genesis 2:17

Who tempted Eve? Genesis 3:1

Who was the serpent? Revelation 12:9

How was Eve tempted? Genesis 3:2-6

What lie did Satan tell Eve? Genesis 3:4

How did Satan attempt to make God look bad? Genesis 3:5

How did Satan appeal to Eve? Genesis 3:6
a. _____ b._____ c._____

LIFE APPLICATION

Did you know that Satan tempts Christians today in the same ways that he tempted Eve?

Read: Genesis 3:1-7.
Satan tempted Eve by causing her to doubt in 3:4.
Satan lied to make God look bad in 3:5.
Satan enticed Eve through her senses in 3:6.

How does Satan cause you to doubt?

What lies does Satan want you to believe about God?

How does he entice you through your senses?

What are the steps that lead to sin? James 1:14-15
a. _____ b._____ c._____

What should you do when you are tempted? 2 Corinthians 10:5

When Adam ate the forbidden fruit, was he deceived? 1 Timothy 2:14-15

How sad! Both Adam and Eve chose to disobey God.

MAN'S DISOBEDIENCE

When did Adam and Eve die spiritually? Romans 5:17

How did Adam and Eve's sin affect all mankind? Romans 5:12

What happened to Adam and Eve? Genesis 3:23-24

The original command of Genesis 2:17 was disobeyed and later God would give new commands to Noah.

SIN BRINGS JUDGMENT

How did God punish the MAN? Genesis 3:17-19

How did God punish WOMAN? Genesis 3:16

How did God punish the EARTH? Genesis 3:17-18

How did God punish the SERPENT? Genesis 3:14-15

How did Adam and Eve die years later? Genesis 5:5

ANIMAL SACRIFICES INSTITUTED

God, in His great love for Adam and Eve, offered the first animal sacrifice to restore fellowship with them. God established the animal sacrifice as the means of "atonement" for sin. The word "atonement" has often been purported as meaning "at-one-ment." Atonement brought reconciliation between God and man. The animal sacrifices served as a temporary covering for sin (Hebrews 10:3-4). They pointed to the "once for all" sacrificial death of Jesus Christ on the Cross to take away sin. Hebrews 10:10,12; John 1:29

God restored fellowship with Adam and Eve by offering the first animal sacrifice and then gave the first prophecy that the Savior Jesus Christ was to come. Genesis 3:15

Why is atonement between God and man needed?
A. _____ Romans 5:12
B. _____ Romans 3:23
C. _____ Romans 6:23

LIFE APPLICATION

Have you received atonement (forgiveness) of your sin? The Lord Jesus Christ died on the Cross for your sin and He came alive again. Trust Him today as your Savior and Lord. See Page 76 for God's Plan of Salvation.

Who was the seed of the woman? Matthew 1:21

Who was the seed of the serpent? Revelation 13:1,2

How did Satan bruise Christ? 1 Corinthians 2:8

How did Christ's death on the cross crush Satan's dominion and headship? Revelation 1:17-18

Read: Revelation 20:10. How good it is to know the end of the story! Christ is the Victor! Satan was conquered at the cross and ultimately his doom is sure in the lake of fire. Satan is a defeated foe!

Name the first two children of Adam and Eve. Genesis 4:1-2
a._____ b._____.

Who did Eve think Cain was? Genesis 4:1. The word "manchild" in the Hebrew could be translated "the Gotten one" or "Man, the Lord."

Who did Eve think was the Man, the Lord? Genesis 3:15

What offering did Cain give to the Lord? Genesis 4:3

What offering did Abel bring? Genesis 4:4

What did Abel's sacrifice show? Hebrews 11:4
a. _____ b._____.

Why didn't God accept Cain's offering? Hebrews 9:22

God gave Cain a second chance to offer an animal sacrifice. Translators offer a possibility for the meaning of Genesis 4:7. It is, "The sin offering is crouching at the door but you must master it." God provided the animal for sacrifice, but Cain again refused to sacrifice the animal.

Go back to Page 3, the Attributes of God. Which attributes of God were evident in God's dealing with Cain in Genesis 4:6-7?

Why did Cain kill Abel? Genesis 4:4-5

Why would Satan want Abel dead? Genesis 3:15

How did God punish Cain? Genesis 4:13-14
a._____ b._____ c._____

What did Cain leave? Genesis 4:16

What did God do for Adam and Eve? Genesis 4:25

Who was Seth's son? Genesis 4:26

What did the family of Seth begin to do? Genesis 4:26

Have you ever wondered why the genealogies are in the Bible? One reason is that they trace the lineage of Messiah, Jesus Christ, from Adam to Mary and Joseph. God had another reason for listing the lineage from Adam through Noah. Through the names of these men, God proclaimed

His plan of redemption through Christ. Look at the names below and read the meanings of their names and then read their names in a sentence to see God's redemptive plan.

Read: Genesis 5. These are the descendants of Adam (followed by the meaning of their names).

Adam lived 930 years	MAN
Seth lived 912 years	APPOINTED
Enos lived 905 years	MORTAL
Cainan lived 910 years	SORROW
Mahalaleel lived 895 years	THE BLESSED GOD
Jared lived 962 years	SHALL COME DOWN
Enoch (translated) lived 365 years	TEACHING
Methuselah lived 969 years	HIS DEATH SHALL BRING
Lamech lived 777 years	THE DESPAIRING
Noah lived 950 years	COMFORT

Why is it important to know the genealogy of Adam? Luke 3:23,36-38

Name 5 things the family of Cain started.
Genesis 4:17 _____
Genesis 4:19 _____
Genesis 4:20 _____
Genesis 4:21 _____
Genesis 4:22 _____

Read: Genesis Chapter 6.
Why was God sorry He made man? Genesis 6:4-5
a. _____ b. _____

In Genesis 6:2,4, who were "the sons of God"? There are two views of who the "sons of God" were: (1) Unsaved relatives of Cain or (2) fallen angels. Read: Job 2:1-2. Notice that the angels are called "sons of God."

"Nephilim" is a word derived from the Hebrew "naphal" and could be translated "fallen ones." The King James version translates this term "giants."

Who were these fallen angels? Jude 6-7

What did the fallen angels do? Genesis 6:2,4

What did this union produce? Genesis 6:4

What happened to these fallen angels? 2 Peter 2:4-5

Once again Satan attempted to thwart the plan of God by corrupting the human race. Why would Satan want the human race corrupted? Genesis 3:15

Why did Noah and his family find favor with God? Genesis 6:9
a._____ b._____

Why did God decide to destroy all mankind and animals? Genesis 6:12,17

What did God tell Noah to build? Genesis 6:14

What was to go in the ark? Genesis 7:2-3
a._____ b._____ c._____

While Noah was preparing the ark, what did he do? 2 Peter 2:5

The name Methuselah means "his death shall bring."

What would come after Methuselah's death? Genesis 6:17

How long did Methuselah live? Genesis 5:27
As long as Methuselah lived, his name served as a warning to ungodly men.

How big was the ark?   Genesis 6:15

Estimating the cubit at 18" (a cubit was a measure from the forearm to the end of the middle finger), the ark was 525 feet long, 87-1/2 feet wide, 52-1/2 feet high.

How long did it take Noah to build the ark? Genesis 6:3

Who was preserved through the flood? Genesis 7:13

Who closed the door after all were aboard the ark? Genesis 7:16

Until this time, how was the earth watered? Genesis 2:6

How long did Noah and his family wait before it began to rain? Genesis 7:10

From where did the flood waters come? Genesis 7:11

How high did the flood waters rise? Genesis 7:20

What was the outcome of the flood? Genesis 7:21

How long were Noah and his family in the ark?

Genesis 7:6 says: Noah was 600 years old when they entered the ark. According to Genesis 8:13-14: Noah was 601 plus 1 month plus 1 day old when he removed the covering of the ark. Therefore, Noah and his family were in the ark 1 year, 1 month, 1 day.

What did Noah do after he left the ark? Genesis 8:20

Since Adam and Eve had disobeyed God's commands, God now gave new commands to Noah.

GOD'S NEW COMMANDS

What did God command Noah? Genesis 9:1,7

How many times did God command to "fill the earth?" Genesis 9:1,7

What was the significance of the repetition of the command?

These new commands established the time of Human Government, when man was to rule over man. It was God's plan that man should scatter throughout the world.

How do we know that the principles of Human Government are still in effect today in the Church? Romans 13:1-2

When city, state, or national laws are disobeyed, who is being opposed? Romans 13:3-4

Why are laws necessary in a nation? Romans 13:4

What other commands did God give Noah?
Genesis 9:2 _____
Genesis 9:3-4_____
Genesis 9:5-6_____

How did God show that He would never again destroy the earth with water? Genesis 9:13-16

In the future, how will God destroy the earth? 2 Peter 3:10

Read Genesis 9:24-27. Name the three prophecies that Noah gave for his sons. What purpose would the descendants of Japheth have?

Japheth and his descendants later settled in Europe. We have been enlarged because we get our knowledge of science, arts, music, and history from Europe.

What purpose would the descendants of Shem have? Genesis 9:26

Through the line of Shem, Messiah was to come.

What purpose would the descendants of Ham have? Genesis 9:25

Who was Canaan? Genesis 10:6

This was the beginning of races.

HISTORY

TOWER OF BABEL

Read Genesis 10:8,10. Ham's grandson was Nimrod. History declares that Nimrod was not only the first king of Babylon, but that he and his wife, Semiramis, began the Babylonian Mystery Religion. The Tower of Babel was built as a place of worship for the various gods of the Babylonian Mystery Religion.

Archaeology reveals that the Tower of Babel consisted of seven platforms with each platform diminishing in size. The top platform was a temple, or sanctuary, and the bottom platform had six gates which led into small chapels.

LIFE APPLICATION

Throughout the centuries, men have worked with their hands to build their own way to God. What does God declare is the only way for us to get to Him? John 14:6; Titus 3:5-7

Why did the people build the Tower of Babel? Genesis 11:4

What was Satan attempting to destroy?

In Genesis 11:3-4, the people said "Let us." What did they demonstrate?

How was this the same as Lucifer's and Adam and Eve's sin? Isaiah 13:14

How did God punish this sin? Genesis 11:9

Who is the "Us" in Genesis 11:7? See Genesis 1:26

How did the nations begin? Acts 17:26

This is the beginning of nations.

MAN'S DISOBEDIENCE

Mankind rebelliously disobeyed God and began worshiping idols. Once again Satan attempted to destroy the plan of God by getting mankind to worship him through their false religious system.

SIN BRINGS JUDGMENT

In judgment, God began human languages, races, and nations to cause mankind to scatter and fill the earth as He planned. Later, God gave new commands to Abraham.

What does this tell you about God's purposes? Isaiah 46:9-10

Turn to the chart on page 93 and locate the GENTILES on the chart. From Adam until Abram, God was dealing with the Gentile nations. Genesis 10:5

HISTORY

The Shemites migrated to Assyria, Syria, Persia, Northern Arabia, and Mesopotamia. Shem's descendants were the Persians, Assyrians, Armenians, and Syrians.

Japheth migrated to Asia Minor, Armenia, and Europe. His descendants were the Gauls, Britons, Germans, Russians, Greeks, Romans, and Thracians. Ham migrated to Africa and Asia. Ham's son, Mizraim, founded the Chaldean Empire on the Euphrates. Ham's grandson, Nimrod, founded the Babylonian empire and his descendants were the Ethiopians, Libyans, Egyptians, and Canaanites.

CHAPTER 2

NATION OF ISRAEL BEGAN

From what nation did Abram come? Genesis 11:31
Abram was a Gentile from Ur.

The book of Genesis is called the Patriarchal, Father, Age. Who controlled the family, including married children? Genesis 11:31

Who served as a military leader? Genesis 14:14-15 (318 soldiers)

Who represented his family before God? Genesis 12:1-3

How did the father serve as the priest for his family? Genesis 15:9-10; 8:20

God changed Abram's name to _____. Genesis 17:5

God changed Sarai's name to _____. Genesis 17:15

How was Abraham made righteous before God? Genesis 15:6

How was Abraham's faith perfected before God? James 2:21-22

What were Abraham and his descendants to observe forever? Genesis 17:10

What was Israel's seal of righteousness? Romans 4:11

LIFE APPLICATION

Did you know that the largest portion of the Bible, from Genesis 12 through Revelation 22, deals with the history of ISRAEL with the exception of the 13 Epistles, Romans through Philemon which tell about the Church?

Mankind, during Noah's day, disobeyed God's commands and later God gave new promises to Abraham. Why was Abraham blessed? Genesis 22:18

GOD'S COMMAND (PROMISE)

What did God promise Abram if he would leave his country and family?
Genesis 12:1-3 a. _____
Genesis 12:2   a._____ b._____ c._____ d._____
Genesis 12:3   a._____ b._____ c._____

God promised Abram that through his lineage the Messiah would come and the families of earth would be blessed through Him.

Why did God want Abram to leave his father? Joshua 24:2

Many years had passed and Sarah and Abraham still had no children so they took matters into their own hands. Abraham took Hagar, Sarah's servant. and she bore Abraham a son. What was his name? Genesis 16:3,11

How old was Abram when Ishmael was born? Genesis 16:16

How many sons did Ishmael have? Genesis 17:20

Who did they become? Genesis 25:16

HISTORY

Ishmael and his descendants made Arabia their home. They became generally known as the Arabians. Abraham was the father of both the Arabs as well as the father of Israel. There has always been rivalry between Isaac (the Jews) and Ishmael (the Arabs) from the beginning and it has continued to the present time.

Isaac was the promised son God gave to Abraham and Sarah. How old was Abraham when Isaac was born? Genesis 21:5

Let us see why it took 25 years from God's promise until Isaac was born.

What did God command Abraham to do? Genesis 12:1

How did Abraham disobey God? Genesis 11:31-32

Abraham did not leave his family as God commanded him. He took his father, Terah, and nephew, Lot, with him. After Terah died and Abraham separated from Lot, then Isaac was born. It took 25 years for Abraham to completely obey God's command.

The name "Isaac" means laughter. Why was Abraham's son named laughter?
Genesis 17:17; 18:11-12

What promise did God make to Isaac? Genesis 17:19

Name the sons of Isaac. Genesis 25:26

The name "Jacob" means deceptive. What new name did God later give to Jacob? Genesis 32:28

How did Jacob obtain his birthright and blessing? Genesis 25:27-34

Why did Jacob regard his birthright in this way? Hebrews 12:16

How did Esau regard his birthright? Genesis 25:34

The name "Israel" means Prince with God and the name "Sarah" means Princess.

Name Jacob's sons through Leah, his wife. Genesis 35:23
a._____ b._____ c._____ d._____ e._____ f._____

Name Jacob's sons through Leah's servant girl, Zilpah. Genesis 35:26
a._____ b._____

Name Jacob's sons through Rachel. Genesis 35:25
a._____ b._____.

Name Jacob's sons through Rachel's servant, Bilhah. Genesis 35:25
a._____ b._____

The twelve sons of Jacob and their descendants became known as "Israelites."

From which son of Jacob was Messiah, Jesus Christ, to come? Genesis 49:10
God promised that through Judah, Shiloh would come.

Who is Shiloh? Isaiah 9:6
"Shiloh" means peace and Christ is the Prince of Peace.

Who was Jacob's favorite son? Genesis 37:3

Why did Joseph's brothers hate him? Genesis 37:3

NOTE:

The coat of many colors was a garment that showed rank and favoritism. Joseph's brothers hated him and perhaps believed that their father would make Joseph the patriarch of the family.

Why else did his brothers hate him? Genesis 37:4-8

What did Joseph's brothers do to get rid of him? Genesis 37:23-24

How did Joseph get to Egypt? Genesis 37:28

How did Joseph obtain power and position in Egypt? Genesis 41:15-33

What did Joseph become in Egypt? Genesis 41:40-44

Whom did Joseph marry? Genesis 41:45

How old was Joseph when he became ruler in Egypt? Genesis 41:46

Name Joseph's sons. Genesis 41:51-52
a._____ b._____

Why did Joseph's brothers and their families move to Egypt? Genesis 43:1-2

What did Joseph tell his brothers about their selling him into slavery? Genesis 45:5
a._____ b._____.

How did Joseph regard his brothers' sin against him? Genesis 50:20

How many of Jacob's family settled in Egypt? Genesis 46:27

LIFE APPLICATION

What application can you make to your life from Genesis 50:20? Think of the pattern we have seen in Genesis. God worked, Satan destroyed, God restored. How can this pattern be seen in the Original Creation? Adam and Eve? Noah? The Tower of Babel? Read: Romans 8:28 out loud. Close in prayer thanking God that He works events, good and bad, in your life for GOOD. God's plans and purposes will never be thwarted.

CHAPTER 3

ISRAEL CAPTIVE IN EGYPT

There is a three hundred year gap between Genesis and Exodus or a total of four hundred thirty years from the death of Joseph to the exodus of the Israelites from Egypt. Read Exodus 12:40-41.

"Exodus" means exit and it records Israel's leaving Egypt. Leviticus records the commands for the Levite priests. Numbers records the numbering of Israel and their being placed into 12 tribes. Deuteronomy records the second giving of the Law.

HISTORY

The Hyksos kings were kind to Joseph because they both were related to Shem and allowed him to become a mighty leader in Egypt. The Hyksos kings were descendants of Shem and so was Joseph. It is thought that these foreign kings were allowed to rule in Egypt because of the new technology they brought to Egypt. They introduced bows, daggers, horses, and chariots which made Egypt a powerful nation.

After the Hyksos kings were dethroned, who came to power? Exodus 1:8

Why was this new pharaoh afraid of the Israelites? Exodus 1:9-10

What did this pharaoh king do to the Israelites? Exodus 1:11

Even before Israel was a nation, what did God prophesy about Israel? Genesis 15:13

What training did Moses receive in Egypt? Acts 7:22

Who wrote the first five books of the Bible called the Pentateuch? Exodus 24:4

The story of Moses is 1/7 of the Bible from Exodus through Deuteronomy.

What are the names of Moses' parents? Exodus 6:20

What did pharaoh command concerning Israelite male infants? Exodus 1:16

How did Moses' mother save his life? Exodus 2:1-3

Who found baby Moses? Exodus 2:5

What did Pharaoh's daughter do with the baby? Exodus 2:9; Acts 7:21

What did Pharoah's daughter name the baby? Exodus 2:10

How long did Moses live in the palace in Egypt? Acts 7:22-23
Why did Moses flee from Egypt? Acts 7:24-29

Did the Israelites understand that Moses was to be their leader? Acts 7:24-25

NOTE:

Moses must have obtained considerable power and reputation in Egypt because Josephus, a well-known historian, said that "Moses commanded an army in the south."

To what country did Moses flee? Exodus 2:15

How long was Moses in Midian as a shepherd? Acts 7:30

Whom did Moses marry? Exodus 2:21; Numbers 12:1-2

Name Moses' two sons. Exodus 18:3-4
a._____ b._____

Why was God seeking to kill Moses' firstborn son? Exodus 4:23-25

Moses, on the eve of delivering Israel, was reminded that without circumcision the Israelites were cut off from the covenant. Why? Genesis 17:10

What was Israel's seal of righteousness? Romans 4:11

Why did the Israelites cry out to God? Exodus 2:23

How did God respond to their cry? Exodus 2:24

Who commissioned Moses to be the leader of the Israelites? Exodus 3:1-6, 10-12

What did God send to enable the Israelites to leave Egypt? Exodus 7:4

NOTE:

God poured out the ten plagues onto Egypt as punishments against the gods which the Egyptians worshiped. The plagues showed that God is the all powerful, sovereign God and these gods were powerless against Him. The Egyptians worshiped the Nile River, the bull, the pharaoh's family, and others. The bull was the most sacred animal and upon its death, was embalmed, stuffed, and was given a ceremony of pomp and splendor.

What was the first plague? Exodus 7:19-20

What did the magicians in Egypt do? Exodus 7:22

What was the second plague? Exodus 8:6

What did the magicians do? Exodus 8:7

What was the third plague? Exodus 8:17

Could the magicians duplicate this miracle? Exodus 8:18

What was the fourth plague? Exodus 8:21

How did God protect the Israelites? Exodus 8:22

What was the fifth plague? Exodus 9:6

How did God protect Israel? Exodus 9:6

What was the sixth plague? Exodus 9:9

How did the boils affect the magicians? Exodus 9:11

What was the seventh plague? Exodus 9:25

How did God protect the Israelites? Exodus 9:26

What was the eighth plague? Exodus 10:14-15

What was the ninth plague? Exodus 10:22

What was the tenth plague? Exodus 11:5

How did God protect the Israelites? Exodus 12:22-24

How did Israel commemorate their deliverance from Egypt? Exodus 12:14,24

What did the Egyptians give the Israelites as they were leaving Egypt? Exodus 12:35-36

At the time of the Exodus, it is estimated that there were about 3,000,000 Israelites.

How long did it take for the Israelites to travel to Mt. Sinai? Exodus 19:1

CHAPTER 4

THE LAW GIVEN TO ISRAEL

GOD'S COMMANDS: THE CONDITIONAL MOSAIC LAW SYSTEM

How long were the Israelites at Mt. Sinai? Numbers 10:11

The time spent at Mt. Sinai was important because the Mosaic Law was given to Israel, the people were numbered and put into tribes, the tabernacle was erected, feasts were instituted, animal sacrifices prescribed, dietary laws given, and baptisms were instituted. There are three parts to the Mosaic Law (1) The Commandments Ex. 20, (2) The Judgments Ex. 21-23 and (3) The Ordinances Ex.24-40. These Mosaic Laws were for the MORAL, SOCIAL, and RELIGIOUS life of Israel. God's intention was that Israel would be holy and "clean" in their moral, social, and religious lives so they could be the light of salvation to the Gentile nations. Isaiah 60:2-3

What was Israel to be? Exodus 19:6

To whom was the Mosaic Law given? Romans 9:4

What did Israel say? Exodus 19:8

Why was the Law given? Romans 3:19-20

a._____b._____

Why was the Law called a CONDITIONAL covenant? Exodus 19:5

NOTE:

Conditional means that IF Israel obeyed they would prosper, but IF they turned from God they would be judged. Read of Israel's sin in Judges 2:13 and how God punished Israel in Judges 2:14. Read of Israel's obedience in Joshua 6:2-5 and see how they prospered in Joshua 6:20-21. This conditional pattern was observed throughout the time of the Mosaic Law.

How long did the Law continue? The Mosaic Law was given at Mt. Sinai and continued until the crucifixion of Jesus Christ. See Page 52, Jesus Christ's relationship to the law and Israel, for how Jesus and his apostles observed the Mosaic Law. The Law covered a period of about 2,000 years.

TABERNACLE

What did God tell Moses to erect? Exodus 25:9

How did Moses know how to build the tabernacle? Hebrews 8:5

Where is the true tabernacle which God made? Hebrews 8:1-2,5

Where did Jesus go after He made atonement for sin on the Cross? Hebrews 9:11-12

What is the Lord Jesus Christ doing in the Heavenly Tabernacle? Hebrews 8:1-2
a. _____ b._____

How did the craftsmen know how to build the tabernacle furniture? Exodus 31:1-3

Before the tabernacle was erected, who served as the priest and offered the animal sacrifices? Genesis 8:20

Who were chosen to be the priests in the tabernacle? Exodus 28:1,41

Who are Gershom, Merari, and Kohath? Numbers 3:17

How were the needs of the priesthood met? Numbers 18:21

What was the tithe? Leviticus 27:32

What else was given to the Levites? Leviticus 7:34; Numbers 18:21

Who filled the tabernacle after it was completed? Exodus 40:33-34

How did Israel know when to begin their journeys? Exodus 40:36

As you look up the following verses, you will discover the different dwelling places of God.

GOD'S DWELLING PLACES

Where did God dwell during Israel's wilderness wanderings? Exodus 40:34

Where did God dwell during Solomon's day? 2 Chronicles 7:1

Where did God dwell during Jesus Christ's day? Colossians 2:9

Where does God dwell today? 1 Corinthians 6:19

LIFE APPLICATION

Have you trusted Jesus Christ as your Savior? Then, God, the Holy Spirit, lives in you.

SABBATH

God established the Sabbath, the seventh day, Saturday, as Israel's day of worship. The Sabbath rest was instituted so Israel would commemorate God's rest in creation.

To whom was the Sabbath given? Exodus 31:13,16

What happened to an Israelite who worked on the Sabbath? Exodus 31:15

When did the early church meet to worship? Acts 20:7; 1 Corinthians 16:2

Why do we worship the Lord on Sunday, the first day of the week? John 20:1-2

FEASTS

God gave the feasts to Israel so they could show their gratitude to the Lord. The feasts were pictures of what Jesus Christ would do for Israel in the future.

1. The Feast of Passover
   The first month of the Jewish calendar is Abib. This month falls in both March and April of our calendar. The 14th day of Abib is the first day of Passover.

   Why did Israel celebrate this feast? Exodus 12:27

   How long did the Passover Feast last? Leviticus 23:5-6

2. The Feast of Unleavened Bread followed Passover. It was a time for the removal of all yeast and leaven (pictures of sin) from the land. It prefigured the burial of the Lord Jesus Christ.

   Why did Israel celebrate this feast? Exodus 12:27

   How long did the unleavened bread feast last? Leviticus 23:5-6

3. The Feast of First Fruits.

   Why did Israel celebrate the Feast of First Fruits? Exodus 34:22
   Crops were planted in November/December and harvested in March/April.

   During the Passover Feast, on what day was First Fruits celebrated? Leviticus 23:10-11

4. The Feast of Pentecost was celebrated 50 days after Passover.

   What was Israel to celebrate? Exodus 23:16

   This was the Feast of the Harvest to celebrate the end of the harvest.

5. The Feast of Trumpets was a feast to praise the Lord for the prophetic future regathering of Israel. Leviticus 23:24

6. The Feast or Day of Atonement, 23:26-32; 16:34. This was a picture of the day in which Israel would acknowledge their Messiah and cry out for Him, cf. Zechariah 12:10.

What were the people of Israel not supposed to do on this day?

What were they supposed to do?

How long did the feast last?

7. The Feast of Booths is called Tabernacles.

How would Israel celebrate the Feast of Tabernacles? Leviticus 23:34,41-43

Tabernacles pictured the time when Israel would be in their own land permanently

8. The Feast of Purim. This feast was not one of the great feasts given by God in the book of Leviticus. It was added to the others in the day of Esther.

Why did Israel celebrate the Feast of Purim? Esther 9:26-28

Have you ever considered how the Lord Jesus Christ fulfilled many of these feasts during His earthly ministry to Israel? The others feasts will be fulfilled for Israel in the future.

On what feast did Jesus die? John 19:14

On what feast did Jesus rise from the dead? 1 Corinthians 15:20. The first day AFTER the Sabbath was the first day of the week.

On what feast did Jesus send Israel the prophesied Holy Spirit to prepare them for the harvest? Acts 2:1

In the future, Jesus Christ will return to gather Israel at the Feast of Trumpets. Matthew 24:31

This will be followed by the Feast of Tabernacles when Israel will be permanently in their land and have their own homes. Amos 9:13-15

ANIMAL SACRIFICES

Animal sacrifices were observed before Mt. Sinai but it was the Mosaic Law that prescribed five specific sacrifices for Israel, two were mandatory and three were voluntary. The sacrifices not only showed gratitude but were a necessary condition to maintain the continued fellowship and mercy of God. The sacrifices also expressed the idea of substitution and propitiation. Substitution is the putting of one thing in the place of another. Propitiation means to regain the favor of God. The animal died in the place of the sinner and the shed blood brought at-one-ment, reconciliation with God. Animal sacrifices were observed continually.

Why were animals sacrificed? Hebrews 9:22

How did animal sacrifices picture the work of the Lord Jesus in the future? John 1:29

Why did priests continually offer sacrifices? Hebrews 10:3-4
a._____ b._____

What did the death of Christ accomplish? Hebrews 9:12

Why are animal sacrifices no longer needed? Hebrews 10:10,12

Why was the trespass offering made? Leviticus 6:1-6, 25
a._____ b._____ c._____ d._____

What offering was given as a voluntary act of worship? Leviticus 3:1

How long was this offering to be made unto the Lord? Leviticus 3:17

What offering showed Israel's gratitude for God's provision? Leviticus 2:1-3

LIFE APPLICATION

The animal died as a substitute for the sinning person.
Read: 2 Corinthians 5:21. Tell how Jesus Christ was our substitute.
What did Jesus take of ours? When we trust Him as our Savior, what does He give to us? This is called the "exchanged life."

Think of the grace of God that we experience today in Christ. As Israel had to continually offer animal sacrifices to keep the favor of God, believers today NEVER will be out of favor with God because of Jesus Christ's "once for all" sacrifice on the cross, Hebrews 10:10. What marvelous grace!

DIETARY CHANGES

Adam and Eve ate fruits and vegetables, Genesis 1:29. Noah could eat fruits, vegetables and meat without the blood, Genesis 9:3-4. Israel was commanded to only eat the "clean" meat, fish, birds, and insects. You can easily understand these different commands by knowing that God gave different commands at different times to different groups of people. Remember, as you read, continually ask yourself to WHOM is it being spoken, WHAT, WHEN, WHERE, and WHY?

To whom were these new dietary laws given? Leviticus 11:2

Where does the term "clean" animals first appear? Genesis 7:1-2

What was the purpose of the "clean" animals? Genesis 8:20

What two characteristics had to be present before an Israelite was permitted to eat an animal?
Leviticus 11:3-4
a. _____ b._____

Name two characteristics of the edible fish. Leviticus 11:12
a. _____ b. _____

What type of birds could Israel not eat? Leviticus 11:13-19

Name two characteristics of edible insects. Leviticus 11:20-21
a. _____ b. _____

God wanted the nation of Israel to be "clean." Why? Isaiah 60:1-3

Leviticus 11   tells how Israel was to eat "clean" foods.
Leviticus 12-13:46   tells how Israel was to have "clean" bodies.
Leviticus 14:33-57   tells how Israel was to have "clean" houses.
Leviticus 15   tells how Israel was to have "clean" contacts.
Leviticus 16   tells how Israel was to be a "clean" nation.

What can be eaten today in the Church? 1 Timothy 4:4

Why are we to pray and thank God for our food? 1 Timothy 4:5

Does God put conditions on what we can eat today? 1 Timothy 4:4

BAPTISMS

The Old Testament was written in Hebrew and the New Testament was written in Greek. The word "wash" in the Old Testament Hebrew is equivalent to the New Testament Greek word "baptize."

Where does the word "wash" first appear in the Bible? Exodus 29:4

What was the purpose of baptism? Numbers 19:9

What nation was given water baptism as a perpetual statute? Numbers 19:9-10

How were Gentiles (foreigners) received into the camp? Numbers 31:19,23

How were the priests cleansed? Exodus 30:18-20

If the priests were not baptized, what happened to them? Exodus 30:21

How was the baptism for purification from sin performed?
Numbers 19:5 _____
Numbers 19:17_____
Numbers 19:18_____

How long were "baptisms" (washings) to continue? Hebrews 9:10-12

Why were washings (baptisms) only needed until Christ? Hebrews 9:12

After Christ offered a "once for all sacrifice for sin" what did He do? Hebrews 10:12

God used water baptism as a visible symbol of the cleansing of Israel from sin. How is our sin forgiven today in the Church? Romans 5:9; 3:24-25

In the future Davidic Kingdom for Israel, how will God forgive sin and impurity? Zechariah 13:1

What did Paul say about water baptism? 1 Corinthians 1:17

Why was Paul glad he only baptized a few people? 1 Corinthians 1:17

There are 5 different words in the Greek New Testament which come from the same root word: bapto, baptistes, baptizo, baptisma, and baptismos. The concordance shows baptizo, baptisma, and baptismos occur a total of 109 times in 91 verses.

Did you know that there are at least 12 kinds of baptism in the Bible? Only five of the twelve are water baptisms. Let us begin the study of the different baptisms. Read the references. As you read, notice WHO is doing the baptizing, WHO is being baptized, and WHY it is being done.

JOHN'S BAPTISM FOR FORGIVENESS OF SIN - (WATER)

Mark 1:4-6; Matthew 21:23-25; John 3:22-23; 4:1; John 10:37-42; Mark 11:29-33;
Luke 3:1-22; Luke 7:24-39; Luke 20:1-8; John 1:15-33; and Acts 1:22
Who is doing the baptizing? _____
Who is baptized? _____
Why? _____

JESUS' BAPTISM TO FULFILL ALL RIGHTEOUSNESS - (WATER)

Matthew 3:13-15
Who is doing the baptizing? _____
Who is baptized? _____
Why? _____

Second Corinthians 5:21 tells that Jesus had no sin but He was baptized to fulfill all the requirements of the Law.

CHRIST BAPTIZING WITH THE HOLY SPIRIT - (NOT WATER)

John 1:33; Acts 2:3-4; Luke 3:16; Matthew 3:11-16; Mark 1:8; Acts 1:3-5; and 11:15-16
Who is doing the baptizing? _____
Who is baptized? _____
Why? _____

PENTECOSTAL BAPTISM - (WATER AND A MIRACLE FOLLOWED)

Acts 2:38; 8:12-18; 8:35-39; 9:18-19; 16:14-15; 19:1-8; 22:12-16; Mark 16:14-19; Matthew 28:19; and 1 Corinthians 1:14-17
Who is doing the baptizing? _____
Who is baptized? _____
Why? _____

DEATH BAPTISM - (NOT WATER)

Mark 10:38-39; Luke 12:49-51
Who is doing the baptizing? _____
Who is baptized? _____
Why? _____

BAPTISM FOR THE DEAD - (NOT WATER)

1 Corinthians 15:29-31
Who is doing the baptizing? _____
Who is baptized? _____
Why? _____

THE TYPE BAPTISM OF NOAH'S ARK - (NOT WATER)

1 Peter 3:18-21
Who is doing the baptizing? _____
Who is baptized? _____
Why? _____

BAPTISM OF FIRE - (NOT WATER)

Luke 3:16; Matthew 3:11
Who is doing the baptizing? _____
Who is baptized? _____
Why? _____

MOSES' BAPTISM - (NOT WATER)

1 Corinthians 10:2
Who is doing the baptizing? _____
Who is baptized? _____
Why? _____

TRADITIONAL JEWISH BAPTISMAL CEREMONIES - (WATER)

Luke 11:38; Mark 7:1-8
Who is doing the baptizing? _____
Who is baptized? _____
Why? _____

TRADITIONAL JEWISH BAPTISMS - (WATER)

Hebrews 6:1-3; 9:10
Who is doing the baptizing? _____
Who is baptized? _____
Why? _____

HOLY SPIRIT BAPTIZING BELIEVERS INTO THE BODY OF CHRIST - (NOT WATER)

1 Corinthians 12:12-14; Romans 6:3-4; Galatians 3:25-29; Ephesians 4:1-4; Colossians 2:9-15; ho
Who is doing the baptizing? _____
Who is baptized? _____
Why? _____

NOTE:

Now that you know that there are 12 baptisms in the Bible, when you see the word "baptism," be sure to ask yourself, "Who is being baptized? Which baptism is it? Why was it done?" The context will determine which baptism is being discussed.

CHAPTER 5

ISRAEL WANDERED IN THE WILDERNESS

The time that Israel spent at Mt. Sinai was very productive. During that time Israel was developed into a nation and God gave them the Mosaic Law system to govern their moral, social, and religious lives. Now, as an organized nation, Israel was ready to again begin the journey toward the Promised Land.

When Israel left Mt. Sinai, which tribe led the march? Numbers 10:14

Where did Israel go after they left Mt. Sinai? Deuteronomy 1:19

How long was Israel at Kadesh? Deuteronomy 1:46

NOTE:

Kadesh was an oasis which served as a camping place for Israel. The herds and flocks remained at Kadesh while different areas of the land were scouted.

What did God tell Moses to do? Numbers 13:1-2

After the twelve spies returned, what did the ten spies report? Numbers 13:31

Joshua and Caleb, the other two spies, gave good reports. What did Joshua and Caleb report? Numbers 14:7-9

How did Israel respond? Numbers 14:10

What happened to Israel because of unbelief? Numbers 14:33-34

While Israel wandered in the wilderness, which gods did they worship? Acts 7:41-43

Why didn't God permit Moses to go into the Promised Land of Canaan? Numbers 20:8-12

How did this show that the Law was conditional?

Who was the rock? 1 Corinthians 10:4

How did Moses see the Promised Land? Deuteronomy 32:49

Describe Moses' physical condition before he died. Deuteronomy 34:7

What happened to Moses on the mountain? Deuteronomy 34:1,5

After Moses' death, where did he go? Deuteronomy 32:50

Who succeeded Moses as leader of Israel? Numbers 27:22-23

What was God's opinion of Moses? Deuteronomy 34:10

After Moses' death, Joshua became the leader of the Israelites.

LIFE APPLICATION

What lessons can we learn from the life of Moses?

CHAPTER 6

ISRAEL CONQUERED THE PROMISED LAND

Israel's 40 years of wandering in the wilderness was over. They reached the Promised Land under Joshua's leadership. Israel conquered the majority of Canaan, the Promised Land. The book of Joshua records the dividing of the land. The 31 kings in Joshua 12:24 are listed as destroyed but there were still small groups of Canaanites, Philistines, Sidonians, and Lebanese which remained unconquered in Canaan.

What did God promise Israel? Joshua 1:6

How would Joshua have success? Joshua 1:7

What miracle did God show Israel? Joshua 3:15-17

How did Israel show they believed God and were ready to enter the land? Joshua 5:5

Why was circumcision important? Genesis 17:10

Name the first city that the Israelites conquered. Joshua 2:1

How many spies did Joshua send into the city of Jericho? Joshua 2:1

When the king of Jericho learned that the spies were in the city, he sent soldiers to search for them. What woman hid the spies? Joshua 2:1,6

How did Rahab show she trusted the Lord? Joshua 2:8-11

What agreement did Rahab make with the spies? Joshua 2:14

How did the spies escape from Jericho? Joshua 2:15-16

When the Israelites invaded Jericho, how did they know Rahab's home? Joshua 2:18,21

How did the Israelites conquer Jericho? Joshua 6:3

How did God reward Rahab? Matthew 1:5

How many nations did Israel conquer? Acts 13:18-19

How many years did it take to conquer Canaan? Acts 13:20

What was God's promise to Israel? Joshua 1:3

NOTE:

Joshua 11:23 and 13:1. These verses can be reconciled by understanding the difference between "inheritance" and "possession." The inheritance was the whole land God promised to Israel but the Israelites only possessed a portion of that land by faith. Israel will possess all the land that God promised to them in the future Davidic Kingdom.

Canaan, the Promised Land, was divided among the tribes of Israel. Joshua 13-21

What method was used to divide the land? Joshua 18:8-10

What was given to the Levites? Joshua 21:1-2

How many cities were given to Kohath and his family? Joshua 21:4-5

How many cities were given to Gershon and his family? Joshua 21:6

How many cities were given to Merari and his family? Joshua 21:7

What were the "cities of refuge"? Joshua 20:2-3

Joshua was ready to die. Name three ways Joshua encouraged Israel.
Joshua 23:6 _____
Joshua 23:7 _____
Joshua 24:19 _____

Where did Joshua write his book? Joshua 24:26

Before Joshua died, what did Israel promise Joshua? Joshua 24:24

CHAPTER 7

ISRAEL EXPERIENCED CYCLES

HISTORY

Israel had no strong central government after the death of Joshua. The older generation who had experienced God's miraculous working in the conquest of Canaan failed to teach their children about God. Consequently, the new generation began to worship the idols of the surrounding nations. Over a period of about 300 years, the book of Judges records 12 cycles of Apostasy, 12 Oppressions, 12 Repentances, 12 Judges, and 12 Deliverers.

Why didn't Israel obey God after Joshua died? Judges 2:10

What did the new generation do since they did not know about God?
Judges 2:11_____
Judges 2:12_____
Judges 2:13_____

How did God feel? Judges 2:14

How did God punish Israel? Judges 3:8

How many years were the Israelites in bondage to Mesopotamia? Judges 3:8

These deliverers were called _____. Judges 2:18

Who was the first judge of Israel? Judges 3:9

How did God empower Othniel? Judges 3:10

After Othniel led Israel to victory, how long did Israel experience rest? Judges 3:11

The other judges were Ehud, Shamgar, Deborah and Barak, Gideon, Tola, Jair, Jephthah, Elon, Abdon, and Samson.

How long did the judges serve as leaders of Israel? Acts 13:20

At the end of the book of Judges, what was Israel's condition? Judges 21:25

LIFE APPLICATION

What lesson can be learned from Israel's failure to teach their children about God and all He had done for them?

How can not knowing God's Word affect your life?

33

CHAPTER 8

ISRAEL WANTED A KING

First Samuel records the ministry of Samuel, the prophet and priest, who served as a link between the book of Judges and the promised Davidic Kingdom.

What vow did Hannah make to the Lord? 1 Samuel 1:11

Who was Hannah's son? 1 Samuel 1:20

How did Hannah keep her vow? 1 Samuel 1:24-25

How did Israel know Samuel was a prophet? 1 Samuel 3:19-20

Why did Israel have victory over the Philistines? 1 Samuel 7:3-4

Why did Israel want a king? 1 Samuel 8:5

Who was Israel rejecting? 1 Samuel 8:7

NOTE:

Israel was ruled by God directly from Heaven until 1 Samuel 8. This was known as a Theocracy. By wanting a king, Israel was rejecting God the Father from ruling over them. Later, they rejected Jesus Christ, God the Son, at the Cross. Finally, Israel rejected God, the Holy Spirit. Acts 7:51

Who was the FIRST king of Israel? 1 Samuel 9:17

What were Saul's human qualifications to be king? 1 Samuel 9:2
a._____ b._____.

How long did Saul rule?   Acts 13:21

How did God empower Saul?   1 Samuel 10:10

Name 3 reasons why God rejected King Saul.
1 Samuel 13:9 _____
1 Samuel 15:17-19 _____
1 Samuel 28:7-8 _____

Who only was to offer animal sacrifices? Leviticus 1:17

Who succeeded Saul as the SECOND king of Israel? 2 Samuel 5:4

How did God empower David to be the King of Israel? 1 Samuel 16:13

How long did he reign? 2 Samuel 5:4

Name the THIRD king of Israel. 1 Kings 2:12

What promise did God make to Solomon? 1 Kings 9:5

How did God exalt Solomon? 1 Chronicles 29:25

What did Solomon do for the Lord? 1 Kings 6:1

What happened after the temple was completed? 2 Chronicles 7:1-2

How many years did Solomon reign over Israel? 1 Kings 11:42

What was the extent of Solomon's kingdom? 2 Chronicles 9:26

Name Solomon's sins. 1 Kings 11:5-7
a._____ b._____ c._____

How did God punish Solomon's sin? 1 Kings 11:11-12

THE HOLY SPIRIT IN THE OLD TESTAMENT

Did you know that the Holy Spirit was not given to everyone in the Old Testament?   See page 61 for a comparison of the working of the Holy Spirit.

How did certain Israelites know how to sew the priest's clothing? Exodus 28:3

Why was Bezaleel given the Holy Spirit? Exodus 31:3-5
a._____ b._____ c._____

What men received the Holy Spirit and why? Numbers 11:16-17

When did Othniel receive the Holy Spirit and why? Judges 3:9-10

When did Saul receive the Holy Spirit and why? 1 Samuel 9:17; 10:9-11

When did David receive the Holy Spirit? 1 Samuel 16:13

What happened to King Saul? 1 Samuel 16:14

Why did David receive the Holy Spirit? 1 Samuel 16:1

Why did King Saul consult the witch of Endor? 1 Samuel 28:15

What did Samuel say would happen to King Saul the next day? 1 Samuel 28:19-20

Where would Saul be after his death? 1 Samuel 28:19

NOTE:

Even though the Holy Spirit had left King Saul, he would be WITH Samuel in Paradise after his death. 1 Samuel 28:19; 31:6

What did King David pray after he sinned with Bathsheba and why? Psalm 51:11

REMEMBER THESE POINTS

When God was dealing with Israel in the Old Testament, the Holy Spirit
(1) mainly came UPON individuals. Judges 3:10
(2) was given to accomplish a certain task. Numbers 11:16-17
(3) was temporary in nature and could be removed because of sin or when the task was completed. 1 Samuel 16:14
(4) was not a seal of salvation. 1 Samuel 28:19

LIFE APPLICATION

How wonderful that today in the Church, the Body of Christ, believers cannot lose the Holy Spirit for He is the seal of salvation until the day of redemption. Ephesians 4:30

WHAT IS THE DAVIDIC KINGDOM?

The Davidic Kingdom is the prophesied time period when Jesus Christ, the LITERAL posterity of King David, will reign on a LITERAL throne in Jerusalem, reigning over the LITERAL Kingdom fulfilling the prophecies made to Israel. It is necessary to understand the characteristics of the Davidic Kingdom in order to understand what Jesus Christ SAID and DID in the Gospels (Matthew, Mark, Luke, and John).

Let us look at the prophecies given to King David about the Kingdom.

What did David want to build for God? 1 Chronicles 28:2

Why would God not allow David to build the temple? 1 Chronicles 28:3

Instead, what did God promise to build for David? 2 Samuel 7:12-13

God told David that Solomon would build the temple. 1 Chronicles 28:6

How long would the throne of David last? 2 Samuel 7:13,16

The Prophets confirmed that Messiah would come through _____'s line. Jeremiah 23:5

Who was related to King David? Matthew 1:1

Who was born to sit on David's throne? Luke 1:31-32

In the Kingdom, over whom will Jesus Christ reign? Daniel 7:14,27

After Jesus' baptism, what message did He proclaim? Matthew 4:17,23

CHARACTERISTICS OF THE KINGDOM

What will be the extent of Christ's Kingdom? Zechariah 14:9

In what city will Christ's throne be? Zechariah 14:16-17

In the Kingdom there will be no _____. Micah 4:3

In the Kingdom there will be no _____. Amos 9:13-14

In the Kingdom there will be no _____. Isaiah 33:24

In the Kingdom, animals will be _____. Isaiah 65:25

In the Kingdom, nature will be under Christ the Messiah's control. Isaiah 35:1

In the Kingdom, there will be _____. Isaiah 65:20

In the Kingdom, there will be no _____ . Isaiah 32:17

So, Israel will dwell _____. Isaiah 32:18

What is the length of the Kingdom on earth? Revelation 20:6-7

To study how Jesus taught about the Kingdom, see: Page 46. Jesus Christ, the King, Proclaimed the Kingdom to Israel. Locate the Kingdom on the chart at the back of the book. What goes before it? After it?

CHAPTER 9

ISRAEL WAS DIVIDED

Name the FOURTH king of Israel. 2 Chronicles 9:31

How long did Rehoboam reign in Jerusalem? 2 Chronicles 12:13

What grievous thing did King Rehoboam and Israel do? 2 Chronicles 12:1

What prophecy was being fulfilled? 1 Kings 11:11-12

What did God tell Jeroboam through Ahijah the prophet? 1 Kings 11:30-31

Who tried to put Jeroboam to death? 1 Kings 11:40

How did Rehoboam treat Israel harshly? 1 Kings 12:13-15

Israel rebelled against Rehoboam. Whom did Israel kill? 1 Kings 12:18

Who became the king of Israel, the ten tribes? 1 Kings 12:20

Who was the king of Judah? 1 Kings 12:23; 2 Chronicles 12:13. Judah consisted of two tribes, Judah and Benjamin.

HISTORY

Israel was divided into two nations. Ten tribes formed the Northern Kingdom called ISRAEL and two tribes formed the Southern Kingdom, called JUDAH. During the divided kingdom, the Israelites were called the "Jus," which was a byword, short for Judah. Later, the spelling was changed to "Jews." I Kings 9:7

Israel, the Northern Kingdom, lasted a little over 200 years. There were nineteen kings who reigned in the Northern Kingdom and all worshipped the golden calf idol. Israel was taken captive by Assyria in 721 B.C.

Judah, the Southern Kingdom, lasted about 300 years and there was a succession of nineteen kings and one queen. The majority of the kings served idols but there were a few who served Jehovah. Even the good kings did some bad things, and the bad kings did some good things. Spiritual revivals were temporary in nature and accomplished no lasting change. The prophets warned Judah to worship Jehovah but they refused to listen and continued worshipping idols. Judah was taken captive by Babylon in 600 B.C.

"There were continual _____ between Israel and Judah." 2 Chronicles 12:15

What evil things did Israel, the ten tribes do? 2 Kings 17:16-17
a. _____ b._____

What happened to Israel because of their sin? 2 Kings 17:22-23

What was Judah's sin? 1 Kings 14:22-24
a._____ b. _____

What nation took Judah captive? 2 Kings 24:12

Who was the king of Babylon? 2 Kings 24:11

What else did Babylon carry away? 2 Kings 24:13-14
a._____ b._____

What did Nebuchadnezzar and his army do to the temple? 2 Kings 25:8-9

What was done to the walls around the temple? 2 Kings 25:10

What country took Israel into captivity? 2 Kings 17:23

HISTORY - MAJOR AND MINOR PROPHETS

Seventeen books of the Old Testament were written by prophets. The prophets were God's spokesmen to Israel and Judah warning of coming events. They prophesied about Israel, Judah, Nineveh, Babylon, the captives in Babylon, and Edom. The books of the prophets are divided into two groups called the major and minor prophets. Major does not mean they are more important than the minor prophets but it refers to the size of the books. The major prophets are Isaiah, Jeremiah, Ezekiel, and Daniel. The Minor Prophets are Hosea, Joel, Amos, Obadiah, Jonah, Micah, Nahum, Habakkuk, Zephaniah, Haggai, Zechariah, and Malachi.

LIFE APPLICATION

God used the prophets to warn Israel and Judah of impending disaster if they did not repent of their idolatry. They refused and were taken into captivity.

How does the Bible warn unsaved people of danger? John 3:36

What danger does the Bible warn Christians to avoid? Ephesians 4:17-24

How are unsaved people captive? Ephesians 2:1-3

What does God want for Christians? Galatians 5:1
a._____ b._____

CHAPTER 10

ISRAEL REBUILT THE TEMPLE

Israel and Judah were taken into captivity by Assyria and Babylon. The Babylonian Empire was conquered by Medo-Persia under the leadership of Cyrus. Cyrus was impressed to learn that his name was mentioned in Jeremiah's prophecy as being the ruler that would permit the Jews to return to Jerusalem.

What did Cyrus decide to do? Ezra 6:3

Who was to go to Jerusalem? Ezra 1:5

How did Judah get money to rebuild the temple? Ezra 1:4

Judah returned to Jerusalem in three separate expeditions to accomplish this task.

What man led the first company of Jews? Ezra 2:1-2

What was the first thing to be rebuilt? Ezra 3:2-3

What did Israel do? Ezra 3:3

What did Israel celebrate? Ezra 3:4

What was built the second year? Ezra 6:15

What man led the second company of Jews back to Jerusalem? Ezra 7:6

The book of Esther fits into this time period.

What did Ezra do in Jerusalem? Ezra 7:10
a. _____ b. _____ c. _____

What caused a revival? Ezra 10:1-3
a. _____ b. _____ c. _____

Ezra assembled and arranged the Old Testament canon.

Who led the third company of Jews back to Jerusalem? Nehemiah 1:1; 2:5

What did the third company accomplish? Nehemiah 2:17; 7:1

LIFE APPLICATION

Read: Daniel 2:21. It says that God lifts up kings and puts kings down which shows that God is all powerful and sovereign. While Israel and Judah were in captivity, God used a foreign king,

Cyrus, to accomplish His plan. Through Cyrus, the Jews were repatriated to their homeland of Palestine. Did you ever have to move to another city where you didn't want to go? What good did God accomplish in your life through that move?

What does the last book of the Old Testament prophesy? Malachi 3:1
a._____ b._____

When Messiah came, what was to happen to Israel? Malachi 3:2-3

How were these prophecies fulfilled? Mark 1:2-4

How was Israel purified of their sin? Mark 1:4-5

NOTE:

We have seen how God the Father has worked in the Old Testament with His chosen, covenant people, Israel. In the Gospels (Matthew, Mark, Luke and John) God the Son came to Israel as their long-awaited Messiah to proclaim that the prophesied Kingdom was "at hand." In the Pauline Epistles (Romans through Philemon) God the Holy Spirit is working in the Church the Body of Christ.

CHAPTER 11

TIME BETWEEN THE TESTAMENTS

The Old Testament ends with Israel back in their land and the Temple worship restored.

HISTORY

The 400 years between the Old and New Testaments are an important time in the history of Palestine. Events occurred during this time period which prepared the way for the coming of Christ.

From 331-167 BC, Alexander the Great conquered the whole world and established Greek cities throughout the empire. Greek culture flourished throughout the empire and the Greek language became the universal language. Later, the New Testament was written in Greek.

The Roman period was from 63 BC to the time of Christ. Rome conquered Palestine under Pompei and Pompei showed favor to the Jews by rebuilding the temple. The Romans were famous for their highway systems. They built roads throughout the Roman Empire and later these roads were used to get the good news of the Lord Jesus Christ out into the world.

NOTE:

Have you ever been to a play? The curtain comes down in the middle of the play and there is an intermission. During the intermission, the stage is changed to a different scene and then the curtain is raised and the play continues with the same theme. This is exactly what happened during the 400 year intermission between the Old Testament and the New Testament. The curtain came down and there was an intermission for 400 years. During the intermission, the scene was changed. The Romans were now in control. The Greek language was the universal language spoken throughout the Roman Empire. Later, the New Testament would be written in Greek. The temple was rebuilt. Roman roads were built throughout the empire. The good news of Jesus Christ later would quickly reach the ends of the empire. Now, the stage and scenery were set for the birth of Jesus Christ, the King of the Jews. The four hundred year intermission was ended and the curtain was raised.

The theme of Israel anticipating the promised King and Kingdom continued.

CHAPTER 12

JESUS, KING OF THE JEWS, WAS BORN

As you journey through the Gospels, you will notice that there are at least four major themes which are woven through Matthew, Mark, Luke and John and are like parallel golden strands which are woven through a fabric. These themes are Jesus Christ's humanity, His message, His relationship to Israel and the Law and His work on the Cross. We will explore each of these themes.

JESUS CHRIST, HIS HUMANITY

Why does Matthew begin his book giving the genealogy of Jesus Christ? Matthew 1:1

An angel appeared to Mary. What did he tell her? Luke 1:31

Why did Mary think this was strange? Luke 1:27,34

Who was the father of her child? Luke 1:35

What did the angel tell Mary to name the child? Luke 1:31

The name Jesus means, "JE"-I AM, "SUS"-YOUR SAVIOR, I AM YOUR SAVIOR.

How did Mary respond? Luke 1:38

What would this child do? Luke 1:32-33
a._____ b._____ c._____ d._____

How did Mary regard Jesus? Luke 1:47

When Joseph learned Mary was with child, what did he do? Matthew 1:19

What did the angel of the Lord tell Joseph? Matthew 1:20

Whom did Mary visit? Luke 1:39-40

How long did Mary stay with Elizabeth? Luke 1:56

Why did Mary and Joseph go to Bethlehem? Luke 2:4-5

Under what time was Jesus born? Galatians 4:4

Who came to see Jesus, the King of the Jews? Matthew 2:1-2

Who was Jesus? Matthew 2:2

Where did the Magi locate the young Child? Matthew 2:11

Name two things the Magi did. Matthew 2:11
a._____ b._____

Why did the Magi bring gifts? Matthew 2:2

Why didn't the Magi return to King Herod? Matthew 2:12

An angel appeared to Joseph. What did the angel tell him? Matthew 2:13

What did King Herod do to the children of Bethlehem? Matthew 2:16

How did God provide for Mary and Joseph's needs in Egypt? Matthew 2:11

How did Mary and Joseph know when to return to Nazareth? Matthew 2:19-20

Now long was Mary a virgin? Matthew 1:25

Name the other children that Mary and Joseph had. Matthew 13:55-56; Mark 6:3

Whom did Jesus say was to be honored? Luke 11:27-28

How old was Jesus when he went to Jerusalem with Mary and Joseph? Luke 2:42

Why did they go to Jerusalem? Luke 2:41

Why did John the Baptist baptize Israel? Mark 1:4-5; Matthew 3:6; Luke 3:3

Second Corinthians 5:21 says that Jesus had no sin. Why did He allow Himself to be baptized by John? Matthew 3:15; John 1:31
a._____ b._____

After Jesus' baptism, He began His public ministry to Israel.

NOTE:

Many commentators refer to John the Baptist as the last of the Old Testament prophets because the New Covenant (Testament) began at the Cross. 1 Corinthians 11:25; Hebrews 9:15

How did Christ take away the Law? Colossians 2:14

As the forerunner of Jesus Christ, what did John the Baptist preach? Matthew 3:2

REMEMBER THESE POINTS

(1) John the Baptist announced the Kingdom was at hand to Israel. Matthew 3:1-2

(2) Jesus was related to King David. Matthew 1:1

(3) John the Baptist baptized Israel for the forgiveness of sins to prepare Israel for Christ's appearance. Mark 1:4-5

(4) Jesus was baptized to fulfill all righteousness and to be identified with Israel. Matthew 3:1; John 1:31

(5) The New Testament began at the Cross. 1 Corinthians 11:25

(6) Jesus Christ lived under the Old Covenant (Testament) and was under the Mosaic Law. Galatians 4:4

CHAPTER 13

JESUS CHRIST, THE KING, PROCLAIMED THE KINGDOM TO ISRAEL

JESUS CHRIST, HIS MESSAGE

The Gospels present Jesus Christ as Israel's prophesied King (Messiah) who offered the prophesied Davidic Kingdom to Israel upon their acceptance. To review the Characteristics of the Davidic Kingdom, see Page 36. The things that Jesus SAID and DID in the Gospels showed Israel what the Kingdom would be like.

The word "gospel" means good news. What gospel did Jesus teach? Matthew 4:23

Jesus preached that the Kingdom was _____ _____. Matthew 4:17

What does the term "at hand" mean?

Where does the term "kingdom of heaven" originate? Daniel 7:27

Who was to reign over all the "kingdoms under the whole heaven"? Daniel 7:13-14

Who was the Son of Man? Luke 9:22

What signs accompanied the message of the gospel of the Kingdom? Matthew 4:23

Why did Jesus heal? In the Kingdom there would be no _____. Isaiah 35:5-6

Jesus chose the 12 men to help Him in His earthly ministry. These men were apostles.

What authority would the apostles have in the Kingdom? Matthew 19:28

Jesus sent the twelve apostles to _____ only. Matthew 10:6

What message did Jesus tell the apostles to proclaim? Matthew 10:7

What was the inheritance of believing Israel? Matthew 5:5

In the Lord's prayer, Jesus told His disciples to pray for the Kingdom to come to_____. Matthew 6:10

Where was the Kingdom prophesied to be established? Zechariah 14:9

Jesus taught his disciples to be "peacemakers" in Matthew 5:9 because in the Kingdom there would be no_____. Isaiah 2:4

How did Jesus show His deity and power? Matthew 8:24-26

In the Kingdom, Christ will control nature. Zechariah 14:17

What miracle did Jesus perform and why? Matthew 9:23-25

In the Kingdom there will be long _____. Isaiah 65:20

What gospel did Jesus continue to teach? See Matthew 9:35. Turn to page 52 for a study of the different Gospels.

Why did Jesus teach in parables? Matthew 13:10-11

NOTE:

The word "Mystery" could be translated secret. Because Jesus only wanted believing Israel to know the mysteries of the Kingdom, He told His disciples stories called "parables" which were secrets about the Kingdom. The unbelievers did not understand these parables. See: Page 85, for other secrets which God revealed.

What miracle did Jesus perform in Matthew 14:18-21 and why?

In the Kingdom there would be _____. Amos 9:13-14

Let's explore how Israel could have entered the Kingdom on earth.

QUALIFICATIONS FOR ISRAEL TO ENTER THE KINGDOM

1. What did believing Israel do with their money to show that they were indeed disciples
   of Jesus?
   Matthew 10:9_____
   Luke 12:33_____

2. Why in the Kingdom, would they be given 100 times what they gave away?
   Mark 10:29-30_____

3. How was believing Israel to abase themselves?
   Matthew 18:3-4 _____
   Matthew 23:12 _____
   Matthew 16:24 _____
   Mark 9:35 _____

4. What did Jesus command concerning eternal life in the Kingdom?
   Mark 10:29-30_____
   Matthew 19:16-17_____
   James 2:24_____

5. What happened to believing Israel if they didn't maintain good works?
   Matthew 5:22,28-29 _____
   Matthew 18:8-9,33-35 _____
   John 5:29_____

6. What did Jesus tell believing Israel about bearing fruit?
   Matthew 7:19-21_____ .
   John 15:5-6 _____

NOTE:

Jesus' followers gave away their money, abased themselves as children of the Kingdom and left family, children, and farms becoming servants of all to prove they believed the Kingdom on earth was ready to begin.

LIFE APPLICATION

We are not required to follow Israel's Kingdom Commands to sell all, leave families or be afraid that our salvation is not secure. Today, Jesus Christ gives new commands for the church, the Body of Christ. Salvation is by grace through faith in the finished work of the Lord Jesus Christ on the Cross and not of works. Ephesians 2:8-10; Titus 3:5-6

Our salvation is secure (Romans 8:39) because God promised (Philippians 1:6) that He will complete the work of salvation.

In our daily lives, how are we helped by knowing Israel's history? Romans 15:4

The Kingdom on earth was planned by God _____ the foundation of the world. Matthew 13:35
The Church was planned by God from _____ the foundation of the world. Ephesians 1:4 We are in the time of the Church, which is Christ's Body.

CHURCHES

Did you know that there are at least four different churches in the Bible? The word "church" in the Greek is "ekklesia" and means a called out assembly. The word ekklesia can refer to any political or religious assembly (church).

(1) Acts 19:32,39,41. The word "assembly" here is the Greek word "ekklesia" referring to a political assembly.
(2) Acts 7:37-38. The word "congregation" is the word "ekklesia." Israel was the church in the wilderness. God, the Father, had His church in the wilderness.
(3) Jesus gave Peter the keys of the Kingdom Church for Israel. Matthew 16:18-19. God, the Son, Jesus Christ, had His Kingdom church.
(4) Paul was given the knowledge of the Church, the Body of Christ. Colossians 1:24-27; Ephesians 3:1,8-10; 1 Corinthians 12:11-13. God, the Holy Spirit, has His Church, the Body of Christ.

SUMMARY

Since there are different churches in the Bible, when you see the word "church," ask yourself which church is it and what people are being addressed. The context will tell you which church it is.

What did Jesus give Peter? Matthew 16:19

These keys were to the _____ church. Matthew 16:19

The keys gave Peter the authority to forgive _____ in the Kingdom and to decide issues. John 20:23; Matthew 16:19

When did Peter use this authority? Acts 5:2-5,8-9

Why did Jesus pronounce "woes" on the Pharisees? Matthew 23:27-28

Why did Jesus weep over Jerusalem? Matthew 23:37

Where will Jesus' throne be in the Kingdom? Isaiah 24:23

What did the apostles ask Jesus? Matthew 24:3

What was to be the next age to come? Matthew 24:21

What are some of the characteristics of the Great Tribulation? Matthew 24:5-7,12,15-16
a._____ b._____ c._____

What people will preach the gospel of the Kingdom during the Great Tribulation? Revelation 7:4

To whom will the gospel of the Kingdom be preached? Matthew 24:14

After the Great Tribulation, what will occur? Matthew 24:29-30
a. _____ b._____

Who are taken away in judgment? Matthew 24:39

As the wicked were taken away in judgment by the flood, so will the wicked be taken away at the Second Coming of Christ.

What does Christ do? Matthew 25:31-32

Who is at Christ's right hand? Matthew 25:33

What does Christ say to Israel, the sheep? Matthew 25:34

NOTE:

The apostles knew the order of events because they were prophesied. The Great Tribulation was to be followed by the Second Coming of Jesus Christ and then the Davidic KINGDOM would be established for Israel on earth.

GOSPELS

Just as there are different churches, there are at least eight different gospels in the Bible. See page 50 for the different Churches. The word gospel means "good news." Let us discover what these gospels are.

(1) Jesus preached the gospel of the _____. Matthew 4:23

(2) What gospel told of the Old Testament and New Testament saints? Romans 1:1-4

(3) What gospel makes Jesus the object of faith? The gospel of _____.
    2 Corinthians 2:12,

(4) What gospel is an aspect of both the Kingdom and Body of Christ? Ephesians 6:15

(5) Paul preached the gospel of _____. Acts 20:24

(6) Paul referred to the gospel of grace as _____ gospel. Romans 16:25

(7) The gospel that was preached to Israel was called the gospel of the _____.
    Galatians 2:7

(8) The gospel that is to be preached to the Church, the Body of Christ, is called the gospel of
    the _____. Galatians 2:7

SUMMARY

Since there are different gospels in the Bible, when you see the word "gospel," be sure to ask yourself, "which gospel and to whom was it given?" The context will determine which gospel it is.

LIFE APPLICATION

Which gospel is to be proclaimed today during the Church, the Body of Christ?
Acts 20:24; Ephesians 3:1-3

What warning is given concerning the gospel of the Grace of God?
Galatians 1:8-9

REMEMBER THESE POINTS

(1) Jesus Christ preached the gospel of the kingdom to Israel only. Matthew 10:5-6

(2) Jesus Christ did miracles which established His "bona fides" as one sent from God. John 2:11; 3:2; 11.47

(3) Believing Israel gave all their money away, abased themselves, left families and became servants of all. Luke 12:33

(4) The twelve apostles were to rule and reign over the twelve tribes of Israel in the Kingdom. Matthew 18:28

(5) There are different churches. Jesus proclaimed the Kingdom church to Israel. Matthew 16:18-19

CHAPTER 14

JESUS CHRIST'S RELATIONSHIP TO THE LAW AND ISRAEL

JESUS CHRIST, HIS RELATIONSHIP TO THE LAW

In which time did Jesus live? Galatians 4:4

When Jesus was born, what Mosaic Laws did Mary and Joseph observe? Luke 2:21-24
a. _____ b. _____ c. _____

Did Jesus teach the necessity of an animal sacrifice? Matthew 5:23

What did Jesus tell his apostles to obey? Matthew 23:1-3

What did Jesus tell the leper? Luke 5:14

What was the weakness of the Mosaic Law? Hebrews 10:4

What was the purpose of the Law? Romans 3:20

What did Jesus say about the Law? Matthew 5:17-18

When did the Mosaic Law end? Colossians 2:14; Ephesians 2:15-16

JESUS CHRIST, HIS RELATIONSHIP TO ISRAEL

To what nation only did Jesus send the apostles? Matthew 10:6

To what nations were the apostles not to go? Matthew 10:5

When Jesus and the apostles ministered to Israel, how did God regard the Gentiles?
Ephesians 2:12
a._____ b._____ c._____ d._____

What message did Jesus tell the apostles to proclaim? Matthew 10:7

Why did Jesus and the apostles minister only to Israel? Romans 15:8

Even though Jesus and the apostles ministered primarily to the nation of ISRAEL, there were a few instances when individual Gentiles were healed because of their great faith.

A Gentile centurion came to Jesus. What did he ask Jesus? Matthew 8:6

What did Jesus command for the centurion? Matthew 8:10

What did Jesus call the Gentile woman? Mark 7:28

What did Jesus do because of her faith? Mark 7:29

What were the Jews not to do? Matthew 7:6

To what nation were Jesus and the twelve apostles to minister FIRST? Mark 7:27

To whom was God's salvation offered FIRST? Acts 3:26

How did God want Gentiles to be saved? Isaiah 60:1-3; Luke 2:30-32

It was God's plan that the Gentiles be saved through Israel's RISE.

CHAPTER 15

ISRAEL REJECTED JESUS CHRIST AT THE CROSS

JESUS CHRIST, HIS WORK

How did Mary prepare Christ for His death? Matthew 26:7,12

Name two things that Jesus told His apostles would happen. Matthew 26:29,31
a._____ b._____

Why was Jesus "grieved and distressed"? Matthew 26:38

What did Jesus pray? Matthew 26:39

Describe Jesus' betrayal and capture. Matthew 26:46-50

_____

_____

Why did He willingly go with the soldiers? Matthew 26:54

After Jesus was captured, where was He taken? Matthew 26:57

What did the disciples do? Matthew 26:56

What did the chief priests and Council do to Jesus?
Matthew 26:65_____
Matthew 26:67_____
Matthew 27:2_____

Who did Jesus say He was? Matthew 27:11

When did Israel reject Jesus Christ as their King? Matthew 27:22-23

How did Israel take responsibility for Jesus' death? Matthew 27:25

Jesus was turned over to be crucified. Describe what the Roman guards did to Him.
Matthew 27:28_____
Matthew 27:29_____
Matthew 27:30_____
Matthew 27:31_____
Matthew 27:34_____
Matthew 27:35_____

LIFE APPLICATION

Jesus Christ suffered all these things for you. He died in your place as your substitute. Have you thanked Him for all He suffered for you? Thank Him in prayer.

What was written on the sign put over the head of Jesus? Matthew 27:37

When did God forsake His Son, Jesus? Matthew 27:46

Why did God forsake His Son, Jesus? 2 Corinthians 5:21; 1 Peter 2:24

Was Jesus killed, that is, His life taken from Him? John 10:18; Matthew 27:50

MAN'S DISOBEDIENCE

Israel rejected Jesus Christ as their King and crucified Him. Jesus Christ fulfilled the Law on the cross and the Law was ended. Colossians 2:14

The New Testament (Covenant) began at the _____. 1 Corinthians 11:25

What happened to the veil in the Temple when Jesus died? Matthew 27:51

NOTE:

The torn veil showed that man now could come directly into the presence of God and no longer needed a priest to serve as a mediator. Jesus Christ is the mediator between God and man. 1 Timothy 2:5 See: Animal Sacrifices, page 24.

LIFE APPLICATION

From Mt. Sinai until the Cross, some 2,000 years, Israel could not obey the whole Law. Think of the years of guilt, frustration, and fear Israel must have felt in not being able to keep the Law! Read: Hebrews 2:14-15. This is why Jesus Christ fulfilled the Law and took it out of the way. How does this personally affect you knowing that you do not have to keep the hundreds of laws obtained in the Mosaic Law?

Who requested the body of Jesus? Matthew 27:57-58

What did Joseph of Arimathea do with the body of Jesus? Matthew 27:60

How did the Romans secure the tomb? Matthew 27:64-66
a._____ b._____

Why were the Romans afraid? Matthew 27:64

What happened after three days? Matthew 28:2

How did the soldiers act when they saw the angel and empty tomb? Matthew 28:4

What did the angel tell the women? Matthew 28:6

Who saw Christ after He was resurrected from the dead?
1 Corinthians 15:5 _____
1 Corinthians 15:6 _____
1 Corinthians 15:7 a._____ b._____

1 Corinthians 15:8 _____
Luke 24:13-15 _____

Name two reasons why the resurrection of Jesus Christ is so important. 1 Corinthians 15:14

a._____ b._____

REMEMBER THESE POINTS

(1) Jesus Christ offered salvation to Israel first. Acts 3:25-26
(2) Gentiles had no hope and were without God. Ephesians 2:12
(3) Jesus Christ, the King of the Jews, was rejected and crucified. Matthew 27:25
(4) Jesus Christ was the "once for all" sacrifice for sin. Hebrews 10:10-12
(5) Jesus Christ is the mediator between God and man. 1 Timothy 2:5
(6) Jesus Christ fulfilled the Law and it ended. Colossians 2:13-14

Did Satan know what Christ would accomplish through the Cross? 1 Corinthians 2:8

GOD'S DUAL PURPOSE IN THE CROSS

God in His great wisdom had a dual purpose which was accomplished by the death of Christ on the Cross. His plan was that Christ would not only reign as King of the Jews (Matthew 2:2) but that He would be the Head of the Church, which is His Body, as well. See: Ephesians 1:22-23. Christ's ruling as Israel's King was prophesied but His being Head of the Church was a mystery (secret). Colossians 1:25,26

To whom was the secret of the Church first revealed? Ephesians 3:8

LIFE APPLICATION

Did you ever sing the song, "Wonderful Grace of Jesus," by Haldor Lillenas? It is one of my favorite songs because it attempts to express the depth of God's grace to us through Christ. The chorus reads: "Wonderful the matchless grace of Jesus, Deeper than the mighty rolling sea, Wonderful grace, All sufficient for me, Broader than the scope of my transgressions, Greater far than all my sin and shame, O magnify the precious name of Jesus, Praise His name."

How do we experience God's grace at salvation? Ephesians 2:8-9

How else do believers experience God's grace? Ephesians 1:3

If you know Christ as your Savior, have you thanked Him for His boundless grace and forgiveness which He has given to you in Christ? For a further study of the Spiritual Blessings given by God on the basis of grace, turn to page 74..

CHAPTER 16

THE KINGDOM OFFERED TO ISRAEL

SURVEY OF ACTS

As you begin your adventure through Acts, you will notice that the Kingdom theme is continued and God is still working with Israel. It is helpful to know that Acts is chronologically arranged and takes us from the Kingdom being offered to Israel to the apostle Paul who revealed the Church. Many changes in commands are observed during the unfolding of this thirty-year period.

JESUS' COMMANDS TO ISRAEL

After the resurrection, what did Jesus command the eleven apostles to do?
Mark 16:14-20

(1) vs. 15

(2) vs. 16

(3) vs. 17

Why was water baptism given to Israel? Mark 1:5; Acts 2:38. See: page 26 to review Baptisms.

Christ gave Israel the commands of repentance, water baptism for the forgiveness of sin which preceded the gift of the Holy Spirit to be followed by a miracle. This pattern can be seen in the following verses. Read the context to determine to whom it is spoken.

Compare:

Salvation	Miracle
Acts 2:38,41	Acts 2:41-43
Acts 4:32	Acts 4:33
Acts 5:14	Acts 5:15-16
Acts 8:12,16	Acts 8:13,17-18
Acts 8:36,38	Acts 8:39
Acts 9:17; Acts 22:16	Acts 9:18
Acts 10:1-2,44-45	Acts 10:46-48

What did the apostles ask the Lord Jesus after the resurrection? Acts 1:6

What was Jesus Christ's answer to them? Acts 1:7

When would Israel receive the Kingdom's "time of refreshing"? Acts 3:19

Where did Jesus Christ tell the apostles to go? Acts 1:4

What was the Holy Spirit to do? Acts 1:8

What prophecy to Israel was about to be fulfilled? Acts 1:4-5

What happened to the Lord Jesus? Acts 1:11

Where did the Lord Jesus go? Acts 1:11

Why did there need to be twelve apostles? Matthew 19:28

What was still being offered to Israel? Acts 1:6; 3:19-20

After Judas hung himself, the apostles decided to choose someone to replace Judas.   How did they know Judas was to be replaced? Acts 1:20

What were the two qualifications needed to be a candidate for apostle?
Acts 1:21-22
a._____ b._____

What two men were qualified to be an apostle? Acts 1:23
a._____ b._____

What man was chosen? Acts 1:26

NOTE:

Paul could not have been a candidate because he did not have these qualifications nor was he even saved until years later.

THE HOLY SPIRIT AT PENTECOST

The feasts were given to Israel to picture what Jesus Christ would do for them in the future. Israel celebrated the feast of Passover yearly to thank God for their deliverance from Egypt. They offered the Passover lamb, Exodus 12:1-10, which looked forward to the time when Jesus, the Lamb of God, would shed His blood on the cross for sin. Jesus Christ died on feast of Passover (John 19:14), He was raised on the feast of Firstfruits (1 Corinthians 15:20), and at the feast of Pentecost in Acts 2, Israel was given the Holy Spirit to prepare them for the spiritual harvest. The next event to occur was the feast of Trumpets, when Christ would have returned to regather Israel. See: Page 22 for further information on the Feasts.

Was the coming of the Holy Spirit PROPHESIED to Israel? Ezekiel 36:26-27

What would the Holy Spirit cause Israel to do? Ezekiel 36:27

What then was Israel to do? Isaiah 60:3

When was the Holy Spirit given to Israel? Acts 2:1-4

What did Joel's prophecy say about the Holy Spirit? Joel 2:28-29

What did Joel's prophecy say would follow the outpouring of the Holy Spirit upon Israel? Joel 2:30-31

The "day of the Lord" is the Great Tribulation and deals with the sufferings that Israel as a nation will experience. Matthew 24:21. For a study of this time period, turn to page 90.

To whose sons and daughters did the prophecy refer? Acts 2:5,14,22,36; 3:12

How did Peter tell Israel they could receive the Holy Spirit? Acts 2:38
a. _____ b._____

What followed repentance, water baptism, and the gift of the Holy Spirit? Acts 2:43. Notice that Peter and the apostles obeyed Jesus' last commands to His disciples before His ascension. Mark 16:16

Why did Peter and John go to Samaria? Acts 8:14-17
a._____ b._____

At Samaria, how did the believing Jews receive the Holy Spirit? Acts 8:17

Where was the Holy Spirit to come? Acts 8:16

How did Israel as a nation respond to the Holy Spirit? Acts 7:51

REMEMBER THESE POINTS

(1) **At Pentecost and in early Acts, God was working with Israel as a nation.**
(2) **Christ still proclaimed the Kingdom to Israel. Acts 1:6; 3:19**
(3) **Pentecost was the "last days" of Israel. Acts 2:14-16**
(4) **The Holy Spirit was prophesied to come to Israel. Ezekiel 36:26-27**
(5) **The Holy Spirit came at the feast of Pentecost and prepared Israel for spiritual harvest. Acts 2:1-3**
(6) **The Holy Spirit came UPON believing Israel after belief, water baptism, and a miracle which followed. Acts 2:38,43; Mark 16:14-18. Compare Acts 2:4 with Acts 11:15; Acts 1:8; Acts 8:16; Acts 10:44.**
(7) **Israel received the Holy Spirit by the laying on of hands. Acts 8:17; 9:17**
(8) **Israel as a nation rejected God, the Holy Spirit. Acts 7:51**

COMPARISON STUDY OF THE WORKING OF THE HOLY SPIRIT

Have you ever compared the working of the Holy Spirit? Let's discover how the Holy Spirit worked with Israel in the Old Testament, at Pentecost, and how He is working in the Church today. Fill in the main points and then compare His working.

ISRAEL IN THE OLD TESTAMENT See Page 35	ISRAEL AT PENTECOST See Page 60	TODAY IN THE CHURCH See Page 80
1)	1)	1)
2)	2)	2)
3)	3)	3)
4)	4)	4)
	5)	5)
	6)	6)
	7)	7)
	8)	8)
		9)
		10)
		11)
		12)

LIFE APPLICATION

Name three reasons why it is important to know how the Holy Spirit works today in the Church, the Body of Christ.

1)_____

2)_____

3)_____

CHAPTER 17

ISRAEL REJECTED GOD, THE HOLY SPIRIT

LAST DAYS OF ISRAEL

What people were in Jerusalem at the Feast of Pentecost? Acts 2:5

What did the Jewish believers in the upper room receive? Acts 2:4
a._____ b._____

What were these tongues? Acts 2:6

Besides Joel's prophecy, where else were tongues prophesied to Israel?
1 Corinthians 14:21

What were the Jews experiencing? Acts 2:17

Pentecost was the "last days" of what nation? Acts 2:5,14,22,36

Describe the "last days" of the Church, the Body of Christ. 2 Timothy 3:1-5

For a study of "The Last Days of the Church," see page 82.

What did Peter preach to Israel? Acts 3:14-15,19
a._____ b._____

If Israel repented, Who would have returned for Israel? Acts 3:20-21

What are the times of refreshing? Acts 1:6

What did Peter tell Israel to do? Acts 3:19

How many Jews repented? Acts 2:41; 4:4

At this time, it is estimated that there were 50,000 Jews in Jerusalem, so the majority of Israel did not repent.

How did the believing Jews try to set up the Kingdom? Acts 4:32

Why were the high priests jealous? Acts 5:16-17

What happened to the apostles? Acts 5:18

What did Peter say when the leaders commanded him not to preach about Christ?
Acts 5:29

What did he continue to teach? Acts 5:30-32
a._____   b._____

What did the apostles think of the flogging they received? Acts 5:41

Describe Stephen. Acts 6:8
a._____   b._____   c._____.

What did Israel do to Stephen as he proclaimed God's faithfulness to Israel? Acts 7:58

Who was Israel rejecting? Acts 7:51

What did Stephen see? Acts 7:56

What did the standing position of God mean? Isaiah 3:13

NOTE:

Israel knew that the standing position of God showed that God was ready to judge because David often prayed for God to "Arise, and take vengeance on his enemies" (Psalms 10:12; 68:1). When Stephen told Israel that Jesus was standing on God's right hand, the Jews angrily attacked and killed Stephen.

Why did God forgive Israel for their crucifixion of Jesus Christ? Luke 23:34

Why couldn't God forgive Israel's rejecting of the Holy Spirit? Matthew 12:31-32

Read: Hebrews 6:1-6.
How had Israel tasted of the heavenly gift (vs. 4)? Acts 2:38

How had Israel seen the power of the age to come (vs. 5)? Acts 2:3-4

Why couldn't Israel be "renewed to repentance" in vs. 6? Acts 7:51; Matthew 12:31-32
a._____   b._____

SIN BRINGS JUDGMENT

Have you ever been to a baseball game and heard the umpire yell, "Strike one. Strike two. Strike three. You're out"? This is similar to what happened to Israel. When they had three strikes against them, they were out. This happened when Israel, as a nation, rejected God the Father in 1 Samuel 8:7, "strike one." Then they crucified God the Son in Matthew 27:22-25, "strike two." They finally rejected God the Holy Spirit in Acts 7:51, "strike three." This rejection was the unpardonable sin which only Israel at that time could have committed. Individuals cannot commit the unpardonable sin today. Israel had rejected the three members of the Godhead and God concluded Israel "out" and temporarily set them aside as a nation.

Through Israel's FALL, God now offered salvation to the world.

63

How long will the partial hardening of Israel continue? Romans 11:25

How does this hardening affect Israel today? 2 Corinthians 3:15

How did God use Israel's unbelief to benefit everyone? Romans 11:11,15

When is this hardness removed from individual Jews? 2 Corinthians 3:16

How will Israel respond when the Gospel of the Kingdom is once again preached during the Great Tribulation? Zechariah 12:10; Romans 11:26

REMEMBER THESE POINTS

(1) **Pentecost was the "last days" of Israel. Acts 2:15-17**
(2) **Israel continually rejected Christ in the beginning of Acts. Acts 4:18; 5:28,33**
(3) **Israel then rejected God the Holy Spirit at the stoning of Stephen. Acts 7:51**
(4) **The nation of Israel was temporarily set aside for unbelief. Romans 11:11**

CHAPTER 18

SAUL (PAUL) WAS SAVED AND BECAME THE APOSTLE TO THE CHURCH

Israel was temporarily set aside. God had worked with Israel from its inception from Abraham until Stephen, and now, because of unbelief, Israel was set aside. How sad! What will God do now? God began His secret plan which He purposed in His heart from before the foundation of the earth. He makes that secret plan of the Church known to Saul (Paul). Let us find out about that plan.

Describe Saul's background. Philippians 3:4-6

Who was in agreement with Stephen's murder? Acts 8:1

What did Saul do to believers in Christ? Acts 8:3; 9:1

Why did Saul want to go to Damascus? Acts 9:2

What happened to Saul on the road to Damascus? Acts 9:4; 22:14

Who did Saul see? Acts 22:14

Where did the men take Saul? Acts 9:10-11

How did Saul receive the Holy Spirit? Acts 9:17

What miracle followed? Acts 9:18

What did Saul do? Acts 22:16

To whom did the Lord Jesus send Saul? Acts 9:15
a._____ b._____ c._____

Saul's name was changed to Paul.

Why couldn't Paul stay in Jerusalem? Acts 9:22-23

Where did Paul go? Galatians 1:17

How long did Paul stay in Arabia? Galatians 1:18

While in Arabia, what did Paul receive? Ephesians 3:6-8

Who revealed the secret of the Church, the Body of Christ, to Paul? Galatians 1:12

Did Paul receive this new gospel from Peter? Galatians 1:12

Who did Paul say he was? 1 Timothy 2:7

a._____ b._____ c._____ .

Who commissioned Paul to be an apostle? 2 Timothy 1:1

Why was Paul sent to the Gentiles to proclaim the Church? Romans 11:14

LIFE APPLICATION

Have you ever noticed that the words Jesus spoke in the Gospels of Matthew, Mark, Luke, and John are often printed in red? Publishers often use red ink to print the words of the Lord Jesus in the Bible because they recognize that Jesus' words are important. Many people consider that the words in red are the most important part of the Bible, but did you know that the Lord Jesus Christ continued to speak after His ascension? He spoke to the apostle Paul and told him the message of the Church. Paul wrote down those words which are the thirteen Epistles, Romans through Philemon. Read: Galatians 1:12; 2 Corinthians 12:1-4. Have you ever thought that the Epistles are Jesus Christ's words too and that they are Christ's love letter to you today?

REMEMBER THESE POINTS

(1) **God commissioned Paul to be the apostle to the Church. 1 Timothy 1:1**
(2) **Paul received the message of the Church, the Body of Christ, from the risen Lord Jesus Christ. Galatians 1:12**
(3) **Paul did not receive this message of the Church from Peter. Galatians 1:12**
(4) **Salvation is by grace through faith, not of works, and is offered to the world. Romans 11:15; Ephesians 2:8-9**

CHAPTER 19

GOD SHOWED ISRAEL THAT THERE WAS NOW NO PARTIALITY BETWEEN THE JEWS AND GENTILES

What did God show to Peter? Acts 10:11-12

What did God tell Peter? Acts 10:13

What did Peter answer? Acts 10:14

As a Jew, Peter ate only "clean" animals as prescribed by the Mosaic Law in Leviticus 11, as did other Jews under the Law.

How many times did God say that the animals were clean? Acts 10:15-16

Why was the command repeated?

What did Peter understand? Acts 10:34

What did God command Peter to do? Acts 10:19-20

Where did Peter go? Acts 10:25

Who was Cornelius? Acts 10:22

What did Peter preach to Cornelius? Acts 10:34-35,39-40
a._____ b._____ c._____

What happened to Cornelius? Acts 10:44,46,48
a._____ b._____ c._____

Why was Peter amazed? Acts 10:45

Why did Paul later accuse Peter of being a hypocrite? Galatians 2:11-13

LIFE APPLICATION

What good news God spoke to Peter! Things such as Gentiles and foods which were previously unholy and unclean to Israel were cleansed because of the Cross. (A Gentile is someone who is not a Jew.)

What is God's plan for Jews and Gentiles today?   2 Corinthians 3:16

How does God see believing Gentiles today? Ephesians 2:19

How wonderful that Gentiles now are offered salvation through Christ! Did you ever eat a ham sandwich or catfish? These are some of the foods that were cleansed.

REMEMBER THESE POINTS

(1) God declared that now food and Gentiles were cleansed. Acts 10:14-15
(2) God now was no respecter of persons. Acts 10:34

CHAPTER 20

GOD REVEALED THE MYSTERY OF THE CHURCH, THE BODY OF CHRIST, TO PAUL

PAUL, HIS MESSAGE

After Paul was saved, he went to Arabia. What gospel did he receive there? Ephesians 3:1-7 See: Gospels, Page 50.

Who revealed the secret message of the Mystery, the Church to Paul? Galatians 1:12; 2 Corinthians 12:1 See page 85 for a study of the Mysteries (secrets) of the Bible.

When did Paul first see Peter and James? Galatians 1:18

How many years passed until again Paul saw the apostles? Galatians 2:1

What did the Jewish brethren want to do to Titus? Galatians 2:3

Did Paul submit to their demands? Galatians 2:5-6

COMPARISON OF PETER AND PAUL'S MINISTRIES

Peter was an apostle sent to the _____. Galatians 2:8

Paul was an apostle sent to the _____. Galatians 2:8; Acts 26:16-17

Peter preached the gospel of the _____ to Israel. Matthew 4:23; 10:7

Paul preached the gospel of _____. Acts 20:24. See Page 52 for a review of the various gospels of the Bible.

Since Peter and Paul had different messages and were apostles to different groups of people, what did they decide to do? Galatians 2:9-10
a._____ b._____

Where did the apostles and the scattered believing Jews continue to preach?
Acts 11:19

Where did Paul preach? Romans 15:20

Did Peter fully understand the new message of the Church that God revealed to Paul?
2 Peter 3:15-16

What does the word "Scripture" mean? 2 Timothy 3:16

How did Peter endorse Paul's writings? 2 Peter 3:16

PAUL, HIS MINISTRY

Who accompanied Paul on his first missionary trip? Acts 13:2

Where did Paul and Barnabas go? Acts 13:4-5

What people did Paul and Barnabas attempt to reach with the gospel? Acts 13:5

What did Paul preach to the Jews? Acts 13:39,43
a._____ b._____

When the Jews refused to believe, to what people did Paul go? Acts 13:46

Read: Acts 13:8-11. What happened to Elymas? How was this a parallel to what happened to Israel? Compare Acts 13:8-11 and Romans 11:10-11,25

Name the kings to whom Paul preached. Acts 24:3; 25:1; 26:1
a._____ b._____ c._____

Israel continued in unbelief. To what people only did God finally send Paul? Acts 26:16-18; 28:28

Paul went on three missionary trips. How many people did he reach with the gospel of the Grace of God? Colossians 1:23

Why were the miracles, sign gifts, tongues, and wonders evident during the early ministry of Paul?
1 Corinthians 1:22; 2 Corinthians 12:12
a._____ b._____

NOTE:

While Paul ministered to Israel, the miracles, signs, tongues, and wonders continued to prove his apostleship, but after God sent Paul only to the Gentiles and the Bible was completed, the tongues, miracles, and signs faded away.

LIFE APPLICATION

Bridges enable us to cross rivers, valleys, and gorges safely. In spite of how useful bridges are, no one builds a house on a bridge because it is unstable and shaky. Houses are built on both sides of the bridge, but not on the bridge. The book of Acts is a bridge taking us from the Kingdom to the Church. Some people build their foundation on Israel's Kingdom side trying to claim Israel's Kingdom promises in the Gospels. Others try to build their foundation on the transitional Acts bridge claiming the "last days" Pentecostal experiences for Israel. Still others cross over the bridge and build their foundation claiming the promises made to the Church.

Where are we to build our foundation today? 1 Corinthians 3:10

What else does the apostle Paul say? 1 Corinthians 11:1; 4:16

What else does the apostle Paul say? 1 Corinthians 11:1; 4:16

Paul built his foundation on _____. 1 Corinthians 3:11

What will believers receive by building on the Church foundation?
1 Corinthians 3:12-14.

REMEMBER THESE POINTS

(1)   **Paul was saved and went immediately to Arabia where Jesus Christ revealed the unprophesied message of the Church, the Body of Christ. Galatians 1:12**

(2)   **Paul did not learn about the Church, the Body of Christ, from the apostles. Galatians 1:12**

(3)   **Peter continued to preach the gospel of the Kingdom which Christ gave to him for Israel. Galatians 2:8**

(4)   **Paul preached the gospel of grace which Christ gave to him. Galatians 2:8**

(5)   **Peter did not fully understand the gospel of grace but recognized Paul's gospel was given to him from Christ and that Paul's writings were inspired. 2 Peter 3:16**

(6)   **Paul did miracles at first to prove his apostleship. 2 Corinthians 12:12**

(7)   **When God sent Paul only to the Gentiles and the Bible was completed, the sign gifts stopped. 1 Corinthians 13:8-10**

LIFE APPLICATION

Do you remember how you acted as a small child? I am sure there were many changes as you matured. God wants Christians to grow spiritually but did you know it is possible to stay a baby Christian? The writer of Hebrews encourages believers to "leave the elementary teachings about Christ" and to go on to maturity. Read: Hebrews 6:1-2. Name the elementary teachings of Christ.
a._____ b._____ c._____ d._____ e._____ f._____

In what books do you read about the elementary teachings of Jesus?

That is right, Matthew, Mark, Luke and John. Maturity comes from knowing what the Pauline epistles teach about the glories of the Cross, the Church, our identity, position in Christ, and many other things. As you study the epistles and apply the principles to your life, you will begin to experience the maturity of which Hebrews speaks. Are you ready to discover more about the Church, the Body of Christ?

CHAPTER 21

TODAY, THE CHURCH, THE BODY OF CHRIST

How can you understand the Bible literally from Genesis through Revelation? Think about it for a moment. Perhaps the most important method for understanding the Bible is seeing the difference between ISRAEL and the CHURCH, THE BODY OF CHRIST. Israel, as a nation, its past and future, was PROPHESIED and the Church, the Body of Christ, was a mystery (secret) and was UNPROPHESIED. Read: Ephesians 3:8-9. The word "unfathomable" in the Greek, could be translated "untraceable" You cannot find the Church, the Body of Christ, mentioned in the Old Testament because it was not prophesied. Locate Israel, then the Church on the chart on Page 93. What are the books of the Bible that talk about Israel? About the Church?.

CHARACTERISTICS OF THE CHURCH, THE BODY OF CHRIST

(1) The Mystery is the UNPROPHESIED message about the Church, the Body of Christ. To whom did God first reveal the Mystery of the Church, the Body of Christ? Ephesians 3:3-7; Colossians 1:25-26

What was Paul's greatest desire? Ephesians 3:10

How do believers get into the Church, the Body of Christ? Ephesians 1:13; 1 Corinthians 12:12-13
a. _____ b._____

(2) Who is the Head of the Church? Ephesians 1:22-23; Ephesians 5:23

(3) Does Israel have any national priority? 1 Corinthians 12:13; Galatians 3:28

How wonderful to know that God is no respecter of persons and that today He offers salvation to all. Romans 11:11,15

How does God see believers today? Galatians 3:26

How does God want us to respond to others? Romans 15:7. Why?

(4) The gospel of the Grace of God is the "good news" that salvation is by _____ through _____ alone. Ephesians 2:8-9

What does God want us to do after salvation? Ephesians 2:10

What are we to do with the gospel of grace? 2 Corinthians 5:20

Why is it important for us to be ambassadors for Christ? 1 Corinthians 3:13-14

LIFE APPLICATION:

Telling others of God's plan of salvation is important. In fact, God wants believers to tell others of God's plan of salvation. Have you ever shared the Lord Jesus with someone? Would you like to? Turn to page 78 and review God's plan of salvation. Ask the Lord to help and guide you. Then share God's plan of salvation with someone and depend on the Lord to help you. Not everyone you tell will trust Christ. Our part is to TELL and it is God's job to SAVE. "Some plant, some water, but God causes it to grow." 1 Corinthians 3:16

(5)   The Unities of the Church.
        The Unities in the Body of Christ are found in Ephesians 4:4-6. Read these verses.
                1 Body
                1 Spirit
                1 Hope
                1 Lord
                1 Faith
                1 Baptism (Spirit), 1 Corinthians 12:12-13
                1 God and Father
                1 Apostle, Paul, Romans 11:13

        In contrast, the number 12 is seen throughout the history of Israel.
                12 sons of Jacob
                12 apostles to sit on
                12 thrones Matthew 19:28, ruling over the
                12 tribes of Israel
                12 gates in the New Jerusalem (Revelation 21:21)

(6)   The Holy Spirit lives IN believers. 1 Corinthians 6:19-20; Colossians 1:27; Galatians 2:20

(7)   In the Church, God UNCONDITIONALLY gives believers all spiritual blessings on the basis of unmerited grace? Ephesians 1:3

God had a CONDITIONAL Law relationship with Israel based on their performance, but today, because of the performance of Christ on the Cross, God in Grace UNCONDITIONALLY lavishes believers with spiritual blessings. Grace is defined as something we do not earn or deserve. See: Page 76 Comparison of God's conditional working with Israel and God's unconditional working in the Church, the Body of Christ.

SPIRITUAL BLESSINGS

As a miner digs to find gold, you also will unearth spiritual nuggets of gold as you look up these verses which describes how God sees you today in Christ. The gold that the miner discovers does not benefit him until he spends it and your spiritual gold nuggets will not benefit you until you begin to use them by seeing yourself as God sees you. Let's begin to dig.

IN CHRIST, believers are UNCONDITIONALLY....

forgiven of all _____. Colossians 2:13

accepted in the Beloved. Ephesians 1:6 (KJV)

_____ in Him. Colossians 2:10

given an _____. Ephesians 1:18

made _____ of God. Ephesians 1:5

made _____. Ephesians 1:1

given His _____ in our hearts. Romans 5:5

given a purpose for living. Romans 8:28-29; 2 Corinthians 4:15-18

_____ into the Body of Christ. 1 Corinthians 12:12-13

there are no_____ in the Church. Galatians 3:28

made new _____. 2 Corinthians 5:17

given the Holy Spirit as a _____. Ephesians 1:13-14

indwelt by the Holy Spirit until the day of _____. 1 Corinthians 6:19; Ephesians 4:30

given power in the _____ man by the Holy Spirit. 2 Corinthians 4:7; Ephesians 3:16

have victory over _____. Romans 6:14

given a _____ to serve the Lord. Romans 12:6

have victory over _____. 2 Corinthians 5:8-9

given _____ life. Romans 6:23

are given God's never ending _____. Romans 8:39

have _____ to understand the Bible. 1 Corinthians 2:12-15

LIFE APPLICATION

God gives believers "all spiritual blessings." Have you ever wondered what a spiritual blessing is? They are blessings which are INVISIBLE and cannot be seen with our eyes but yet are very real. Some of the INVISIBLE spiritual blessings are listed above. In comparison, Israel's blessings were VISIBLE and were things they could SEE and DO such as the animal sacrifices, miracles, conquering the land, the tabernacle, feasts, circumcision, baptisms, etc. The spiritual blessings are how God sees YOU IN CHRIST today. Think of it! He says, "you are a saint, complete in Him, accepted in the Beloved, forgiven of all sin" and so on. As you believe these facts about yourself and daily affirm, "I AM a saint, I AM a child of God, I AM a new creation and ALL MY SINS ARE FORGIVEN," watch your IDENTITY, PURPOSE, and CONFIDENCE grow! Philippians 4:8-9. The more you practice these principles, the more it will become a pattern of your life and you will experience increasing victory over the world, flesh and the devil.

REMEMBER THESE POINTS

(1) **The Mystery is the secret message of the Church. Colossians 1:25-26**
(2) **The Mystery was first revealed to the Apostle Paul. Ephesians 3:8**
(3) **Christ is the Head of the Body. Ephesians 1:22-23**
(4) **Israel has no national priority. 1 Corinthians 12:13; Galatians 3:28**
(5) **Salvation is by Grace through Faith alone. Ephesians 2:8-9**
(6) **The Church has seven unities. Ephesians 4:4-6**
(7) **The Holy Spirit lives IN believers. 1 Corinthians 6:19-20**
(8) **Believers have all spiritual blessings. Ephesians 1:3**

GOD'S PLAN OF SALVATION

If you have never trusted Jesus Christ as your personal Savior, you can today. ***None of us can be good enough to meet God's perfect standard of holiness because the Bible says, "We all have sinned and fall short of the glory of God." Romans 3:23

Our sin separates us from a holy God and we deserve to be punished forever. Romans 6:23 says, "The wages of sin is death."

The Good News is that God loved us while we were sinners and He sent His Son, Jesus Christ, who took the punishment of our sin. He died in our place as our substitute so we would not be punished for our sin. "God demonstrated His own love for us, in that while we were yet sinners, Christ died for us" Romans 5:8

Do you believe the FACTS that Jesus Christ DIED for your sin and that HE AROSE from the dead? Prayer is a way to tell God that you are TRUSTING in Jesus Christ ALONE as your Savior. Why not tell God now

> that you are a sinner and deserve to be punished,
> that you believe Jesus died for your sin and that He arose from the dead,
> that you thank Him for forgiving your sins, and
> that you are trusting Jesus alone as your Savior.

After you have prayed and trusted Him as your Savior and Lord, tell someone of your decision. Read: Romans 10:9-10. Then live for the Lord by pleasing Him in all you do and say.

In your adventure through the Bible, you already have looked up many verses about Israel and the Church. This chart is a concise way for you to compare Israel under the Law and the Church under Grace in a simple format. Look up the verses to see the different commands between Israel and the Church.

K I N G D O M -Conditional I S R A E L-Law	C H U R C H-Grace Unconditional
Israel was forgiven only IF they forgave. Luke 17:3; Matthew 18:27-35	Believers are forgiven of ALL sin. Colossians 2:13; Ephesians 1:7
Prayers were answered according to THEIR WILL and IF they had faith. John 14:12-14; 15:7,16; Mark 11:24; Matthew 17:20;18:19-20; 21:21-23	Prayers answered according to GOD'S WILL. Romans 8:26-27
Israel received the amount they gave. Mark 4:24; Luke 6:38	Blessed with all spiritual blessings because of the Cross. Ephesians 1:3

Israel was judged by how they judged others. Matthew 7:1-2; 12:36-37; Luke 6:37	No judgment for sin because Jesus Christ was punished as the sinner's substitute. Romans 8:1; 1 Peter 2:24; 2 Corinthians 5:21

Healing and miracles conditional upon Israel's belief. Mark 9:23-25; Luke 17:19; Matthew 13:58	While Paul ministered to Israel, he had the signs of an apostle doing miracles. 2 Corinthians 12:12; Acts 19:11-12. After God sent him to the Gentiles, healing according to GOD'S WILL. - Paul ill, prayed 3 times but not healed. 2 Corinthians 12:7-10 - Timothy, a man of sincere faith, not healed. 2 Timothy 1:5; 1 Timothy 5:23 - Paul leaves Trophimus sick at Miletum. 2 Timothy 4:20 - In mercy, God healed Epaphroditis. Philippians 2:25-26 - The Holy Spirit gives strength in inner man. 2 Corinthians 4:7 - His power is made perfect in our weakness. 2 Corinthians 12:9

Christ's relationship with Israel was Master and Servant and was based on their deeds. Failure to obey brought loss of salvation. John 15:5-6; Matthew 24:45-51; Matthew 7:22-23	Believers are sons of God. Romans 8:16-17. Failure of son: 1 Corinthians 5:5; 3:15. Loss of reward but not loss of salvation. Believers are children, heirs of God, fellow-heirs with Christ. Romans 8:17

LIFE APPLICATION

How can knowing that God has different commands for Israel than He does for the Church help you in a practical way? Yes, God's grace is beautiful! Have you thanked Him for His unmerited grace to you through Christ?

G-God's
R-Redemption
A-At
C-Christ's
E-Expense

THE HOLY SPIRIT IN THE CHURCH

How and when is the Holy Spirit received? Ephesians 1:13-14

Is any other work (something we do) required? Romans 4:5; Ephesians 2:8-9;
Titus 3:5-6; 2 Timothy 1:9

Why is the Holy Spirit given to believers? 2 Corinthians 5:5

What relationship do believers have with God? Romans 8:15-16

Where does the Holy Spirit place believers? 1 Corinthians 12:13

This union makes a believer a member of _____, the Church. 1 Corinthians 12:27

The Holy Spirit places believers IN Christ. Notice how many times Paul in the epistles describes believers as being In HIM or IN CHRIST. The term IN CHRIST refers to the corporate Church, the Body of Christ. Those who are IN CHRIST are _____ by God. Ephesians 1:4

NOTE:

Airplanes have determined (predestined) destinations to certain cities and unless there is an accident, the planes will arrive at their predetermined destinations. The person deciding to fly to a certain city will purchase a ticket and then board the plane. The person is not predestined. It is the plane that is predestined and the person by being on that plane will get to that city. This illustration will perhaps help you to understand that like the plane, the Church, the Body of Christ, is predestined for Heaven. A person must decide whether they want to go to Heaven by trusting Christ alone as his/her Savior. Upon belief, the Holy Spirit baptizes the person INTO the Church. (Romans 10:9-10; 1 Corinthians 12:12-13). The person is not predestined. It is the Church that is predestined and the person by being IN HIM, the Church, is predestined for Heaven.

Name four ways the indwelling Holy Spirit helps us.

2 Corinthians 4:7_____
Romans 6:6_____
1 Corinthians 2:12-13_____
Romans 5:5_____

How are we to be led in the Christian life? Romans 8:14

How do we know we are walking in the Spirit? Ephesians 5:9-11
a._____ b._____

What fruit will be evident in our lives when the Holy Spirit is at work in us? Galatians 5:22-23
a._____ b._____ c._____ d._____ e._____
f._____ g._____ h._____ i._____

How does the Holy Spirit help you study the Bible? John 14:26
a_____ b._____

The Holy Spirit doesn't bring attention to Himself. Who does the Holy Spirit glorify?
John 16:14

When do we experience the power of the Holy Spirit? 2 Corinthians 12:9

What did Paul say about his weaknesses? 2 Corinthians 12:9

How does the Holy Spirit help us when we pray? Romans 8:26-27
a._____ b._____

What does God accomplish with the various circumstances and trials in our
lives? Romans 8:28-29
a. _____ b._____

What does the Holy Spirit give believers? Ephesians 4:8

Does everyone have the same gifts? Romans 12:6

What is the purpose of these gifts? Ephesians 4:12

Believers lives are _____ when they are not obeying the Lord. 1 Corinthians 3:3

A fleshly life is when we are living to please ourselves and not the Savior and it _____ and
_____ the Holy Spirit. Ephesians 4:30, 1 Thessalonians 5:19 (Quenching means that His
power is choked out within us).

How does God want believers to be? Ephesians 5:1-2
a._____ b._____ c._____

How can believers know they are walking in the Spirit?
Ephesians 4:24_____
Ephesians 4:25_____
Ephesians 4:26-27_____
Ephesians 4:28_____
Ephesians 4:29_____
Ephesians 4:31_____
Ephesians 4:32_____
Ephesians 4:15_____

How does Satan appear? 2 Corinthians 11:14

Is our warfare against people? Ephesians 6:12

Where does warfare against Satan occur? 2 Corinthians 10:5

What is the goal for believers? 2 Corinthians 10:5

Who are we to please? 1 Thessalonians 4:1; Romans 15:1-2

Why? Romans 15:3

How do believers have victory over Satan?
Ephesians 6:13_____
Ephesians 6:16_____
Ephesians 6:17_____

How are believers to influence their world for Christ? Ephesians 5:10-12
a._____b._____

Do you know that the Holy Spirit will stay in our lives? Philippians 1:6; Ephesians 4:30

"The day of redemption" and "the day of Jesus Christ" is the time when Christ comes for believers at the Rapture or death.

REMEMBER THESE POINTS

In the Church, the Body of Christ the believer has an intimate relationship with the Holy Spirit.

  (1)   The Holy Spirit is given at salvation. Ephesians 1:13-14
  (2)   The Holy Spirit puts believers IN CHRIST, which is the corporate Church, the Body of Christ. Ephesians 1:4
  (3)   The Holy Spirit is a seal of salvation. 2 Corinthians 1:22
  (4)   The Holy Spirit lives IN believers. 1 Corinthians 6:19-20
  (5)   The Holy Spirit can be quenched or grieved. Ephesians 4:30; 1 Thessalonians 5:19
  (6)   The Holy Spirit gives power over sin. Romans 6:6
  (7)   The Holy Spirit helps us in prayer. Romans 8:26-27
  (8)   The Holy Spirit guides us. Romans 8:13-14
  (9)   The Holy Spirit teaches us the Bible. 1 Corinthians 2:12-15
  (10)   The Holy Spirit empowers us. Romans 15:13
  (11)   The Holy Spirit is permanent until the day of redemption. Ephesians 4:30
  (12)   The Holy Spirit empowers us. 2 Corinthians 12:9

LIFE APPLICATION

Most of us have automobiles or know of someone who does. The automobile is designed with a motor which gives it the power to move. We can either push the car to make it move or we can use the key to start the engine which will propel the automobile. The same is true in the spiritual realm as well. We can choose to live self-controlled lives which results in sorrow, frustration, and fear, or we can choose to live Spirit-filled lives which leads to peace and joy. Read: Romans 15:13. Have you experienced that peace and joy that comes from being controlled by the Holy Spirit? Filling of the Holy Spirit is like breathing. When we breathe, we EXHALE and then we INHALE. Spiritually EXHALE, by admitting sin to God, such as anger, not forgiving, fear, and thank Him that Christ died for that sin. We INHALE by asking God to break those sin patterns in our lives and asking Him to fill us with the Holy Spirit. His peace and joy will return. Practice spiritual breathing when you lack peace and joy.

CHAPTER 22

THE RAPTURE OF THE CHURCH

LAST DAYS OF THE CHURCH

Describe the LAST DAYS of the Church. 2 Timothy 3:1-7

How does the present time of Grace end? 1 Thessalonians 4:16-18; 1 Corinthians 15:51-53

Read: 1 Thessalonians 4:17. The Latin word for "caught up" is "Rapto." From this Latin word, we get the word "Rapture" which is the event of the catching away of the Church.

How fast does the Rapture happen? 1 Corinthians 15:52

What happens to living believers at the Rapture? 1 Thessalonians 4:17

What happens to the dead in Christ? 1 Thessalonians 4:16

What sounds will be heard? 1 Thessalonians 4:16

How will believers be changed? Philippians 3:20-21

What is the destination of the Church? Ephesians 1:3; 2:6; 3:10; 6:9; Colossians 1:5

NOTE:

The term "heavenly places" could be translated the heavens above the heavens.

What is another name given for the Church? Romans 11:25

We are in the "fullness of the Gentiles" which lasts until the Church, the Body of Christ, is finished, complete, or full.

What is called the fullness of Christ? Ephesians 1:22-23

LIFE APPLICATION

God determined and knows the future. Where does He already see believers?
Ephesians 2:6

What will believers be doing there? 1 Corinthians 6:2-3

In the ages to come, what does God want to show believers? Ephesians 2:7

You are ready for the Rapture if you have trusted Jesus Christ as your Savior and Lord.

How does contemplating Christ's return help us?

How can anticipating Christ's return have a purifying affect on our lives? 1 John 3:2-3

What happens to the Body of Christ after the Rapture? 2 Timothy 4:1

.

CHAPTER 23

THE JUDGMENT (BEMA) SEAT OF CHRIST FOR REWARDS FOR SAVED

The Judgment Seat of Christ is an expression that appears only in Romans through Philemon and it is where believers are rewarded. The words "Judgment Seat" are translated from the Greek word "Bema" meaning an official judge's seat. It is not the usual word "krisis" which means punishment.

How good it is to know that believers never receive God's punishment (krisis) for sin, because it has already fallen on the believer's substitute, the Lord Jesus Christ, on the Cross. 2 Corinthians 5:21

What does Jesus say in John 3:18?
The word "judged" is translated from the Greek word "krisis."

Is a believer ever judged (condemned)? Romans 8:1

NOTE:

The White Throne Judgment is for the penalty of sin which is meted out on unbelievers. See: White Throne Judgment, page 94.

To whom is 2 Corinthians addressed? 2 Corinthians 1:1

Who appears before the Bema Seat? 2 Corinthians 5:10

What is the purpose of the Judgment Seat of Christ? 1 Corinthians 3:12-14

Why is the Judgment Seat of Christ necessary? 1 Corinthians 4:4-5

The Greek word for crown is "Diadem" and could be translated "gold crown." The other word for "crown" is "stephanos." A stephanos crown was a garland or wreath placed on the head of a winning athlete. Believers will be given the stephanos crowns of glory.

Name the crowns of glory and why these crowns are given?
2 Timothy 4:8
1 Thessalonians 2:19-20
James 1:12
Revelation 2:10
1 Corinthians 9:24-25

LIFE APPLICATION

As team members of the Church, we will all be rewarded at the Bema Seat for our own performance, our special work in the Church. Praise from people on earth is shallow in comparison to the approval God will give believers.

Read: Colossians 3:23-24. What work will be rewarded? We are rewarded for the small as well as large things we do for the Lord.

Who is at work in believers? Philippians 2:13

Who will ultimately get the glory for the good done in our lives? Ephesians 1:6,12,14

MYSTERIES (SECRETS) OF THE BIBLE

Have you ever had something good happen to you but you decided to keep it a secret until the appropriate time and then reveal it? Well, God also has had secrets which He has kept in His heart until the proper time. The Bible calls these secrets "Mysteries." Read: Ephesians 3:3-6.

What are some of these mysteries?
Romans 11:25_____
Ephesians 3:3-7_____
Colossians 1:27_____
2 Thessalonians 2:7_____
1 Timothy 3:9_____
Matthew 13:10-11_____

In the context of rewards, what are believers to do? 1 Corinthians 4:1-2

NOTE:
Consistent and diligent Bible study is vital to receive this reward. It requires a careful study of the Bible observing the distinctions between Israel and the Church. 2 Timothy 2:15

The knowledge of God's Word, the Bible, is not only for a select few but it is meant for everyone. What does God want us to do? Colossians 1:10
a._____ b._____ c._____

LIFE APPLICATION

Yes, God has a purpose for our lives and we will be rewarded. Have you ever considered that your rewards and glory in heaven depend on how you have served Him here on earth? How has the study of rewards impacted your life?

CHAPTER 24

THE GREAT TRIBULATION FOR ISRAEL FOLLOWS THE RAPTURE OF THE CHURCH

What are some of the names given to this Great Tribulation time?
Matthew 24:21_____
Jeremiah 30:7_____
2 Thessalonians 2:2; 2 Peter 3:10_____
Revelation 6:16-17_____
Daniel 9:24-27_____

The purpose of the Tribulation period.

(1) The Great Tribulation is a time when God IN HEAVEN pours the seals, bowls, and trumpet judgments onto the earth to punish Antichrist and his followers. Revelation 6 (Seals), Revelation 8 (Trumpets), and Revelation 16 (Bowls).

(2) The Great Tribulation is the time God punishes the nations for their treatment of Israel. Ezekiel 38:22-23; Revelation 19:14-21

(3) The Great Tribulation is a time when Satan kills believers in Christ, counterfeits the works of Christ on the EARTH to deceive men, and attempts to finally win the conflict of the ages between Christ and himself. Satan's working is through the unholy trinity: the Dragon (Satan), representing God the Father, Revelation 13:2, the Antichrist (Beast), representing Christ, Revelation 19:20, and the False Prophet, representing the Holy Spirit, Revelation 19:20.

NOTE:

The Church, the Body of Christ, is not found in the book of Revelation because it records the day of Jacob's Trouble for Israel.

How does Satan deceive those who are living on the earth? Revelation 13:14

What does Satan do? 2 Thessalonians 2:4
a._____ b._____

What does Satan do to the people who do not worship his image? Revelation 13:15

What gospel will be proclaimed during the Tribulation? Matthew 24:14

It is the same gospel the _____ and His _____ preached. Matthew 4:23; Matthew 10:5-6

What prayer will Israel once again pray during this tribulation time? Matthew 6:10-13. "Evil" could be translated the evil one.

What happens to those who do not take the mark of the Antichrist? Revelation 7:14

Name two reasons why Israel must be faithful until death. Revelation 2:10; Matthew 24:13
a._____ b._____.

What will be given to those who overcome? Revelation 3:5
a._____ b._____

What is one of the first things Antichrist will do? Daniel 9:27

What happens after 3-1/2 years?
a. Daniel 9:27_____
b. Daniel 11:31 _____
c. Daniel 11:36 _____

How does the Great Tribulation end? Matthew 24:30

NOTE:

Israel never received the Kingdom on earth because of unbelief but at the Second Coming, Christ will present Himself to Israel, show them the nailprints in His hands and they, corporately as a nation, will believe on Jesus Christ as their Messiah. Zechariah 12:10; Romans 11:26

REMEMBER THESE POINTS

(1)   **The Church, the Body of Christ, is raptured and taken to Heaven. 1 Thessalonians 4:17**

(2)   **The Antichrist makes a covenant with Israel. Daniel 9:27**

(3)   **After 3-1/2 years, Antichrist puts an end to the animal sacrifices. Daniel 9:27**

(4)   **Antichrist seats himself in the temple saying he is god. 2 Thessalonians 2:4**

(5)   **Anyone who resists Antichrist and does not receive the mark of the beast, will be killed. Revelation 7:14**

(6)   **At the end of the Great Tribulation, Christ returns and stands on the Mt. of Olives. Acts 1:11; Zechariah 14:4.**

CHAPTER 25

JESUS CHRIST'S SECOND COMING FOR ISRAEL TO THE MOUNT OF OLIVES

Jesus Christ returns and is victorious over Satan at the end of the Great Tribulation. Name two things that Jesus Christ, the Messiah, does to unbelievers. Matthew 24:30, 39
a._____ b._____

How does Israel respond? Matthew 24:30

Describe Jesus Christ's appearance when He returns. Revelation 19:11-16
a._____ b._____ c._____ d._____

What is Israel's response to Christ at His second coming?
Zechariah 12:10 _____
Romans 11:26_____

When Jesus Christ returns, what does He bring with Him? Revelation 22:12

Remember! The members of the Body of Christ, the Church, are promised the heavens above the heavens in Ephesians 1:3,20 and already have been rewarded at the Bema Seat of Christ. See page 84

What happens after Jesus Christ's return? Revelation 19:19

What is the name of this war? Revelation 16:16
"Har-Magedon" is transliterated Armageddon.

Where will the battle of Armageddon be fought? Zechariah 12:11

After the battle of Armageddon, what will happen to Satan? Revelation 20:2-3

How long is Satan imprisoned? Revelation 20:7

NOTE:

Christ now is ready to set up His earthly Kingdom.

CHAPTER 26

DAVIDIC KINGDOM ESTABLISHED TO FULFILL PROPHECIES MADE TO ISRAEL

After Satan is imprisoned, what does Jesus Christ do? Revelation 20:4

How long does Jesus Christ reign? Revelation 20:4

Christ fulfills all the promises made to Israel in the Old Testament and the Gospels regarding the Davidic Kingdom on earth.

Who will rule with Christ? Revelation 20:4

What will Israel inherit? Matthew 25:34

What is the extent of the Kingdom? Zechariah 14:9

For a detailed description of the Davidic Kingdom, see: page 37

What does God promise Israel? Ezekiel 39:28-29
a._____ b._____ c._____

What does God build for Israel? Ezekiel 40:5

Where will Christ dwell in the Kingdom? Ezekiel 43:7

What will be the position of the temple? Isaiah 2:2

This is the Millennial Temple which will be built during the thousand-year reign of Jesus Christ on the earth.

Who cannot enter the Temple? Ezekiel 44:9

What again will be observed? Ezekiel 44:15

What will be the duties of the priests? Ezekiel 44:24
a._____ b._____

What days will Israel again observe? Ezekiel 44:24

For 1,000 years Christ will rule over the whole earth. Israel will be in their land. There will be peace, safety and prosperity.. The Millennial Temple will be built and there Christ will dwell. The priesthood, animal sacrifices, feasts, and Sabbaths will again be established.

At the end of the one thousand years, what happens to Satan? Revelation 20:7

How does God judge Satan and the deceived nations? Revelation 20:8-9

What happens to Satan, the False Prophet, and the Beast? Revelation 20:10

LIFE APPLICATION

The conflict of the ages between God and Satan is over. Christ is the Victor! Satan, the False Prophet, and the Beast are doomed in the lake of fire forever and ever. What difference does it make in your life today knowing that Jesus Christ is the victor who controls the future?

CHAPTER 27

WHITE THRONE JUDGMENT OF THE UNSAVED

When does the White Throne Judgment occur? Revelation 20:10-11

The White Throne Judgment is where the penalty for sin is meted out on unbelievers.

Who stands before the White Throne for judgment? Revelation 20:12

How will unbelievers be judged? Revelation 20:12-13

What happens when their names are not found in the Lamb's Book of Life? Revelation 20:15

What book records the names of believers in Christ? Philippians 4:1-3

What determines the amount of punishment the unsaved will receive in the lake of fire?
Revelation 20:12

NOTE:

God is fair. The unsaved will be judged by their works for what they have done on earth.

What is the second death? Revelation 21:8

LIFE APPLICATION

We will all stand before Jesus Christ one day, either at the Bema Seat to be rewarded as a
believer, or we will stand before Him as our Judge for eternal punishment of our sins at the White
Throne Judgment. Where will you appear? If you do not know Jesus Christ as your Savior, turn
to page 76, God's Plan of Salvation.

CHAPTER 28

NEW HEAVEN, NEW EARTH, AND THE NEW JERUSALEM

Have you ever read the last chapter of a book first so you could see how the story ends? Revelation 19:11-21 tells how Christ wins the battle and is exalted as King of kings and Lord of lords.

What honor will Jesus Christ be given? Philippians 2:9-11
a._____ b._____

Name two things that Christ conquered. Revelation 1:17-18
a._____ b._____

What follows the White Throne Judgment? Ephesians 1:10

What new things does God make? Revelation 21:1-2
a._____ b._____ c._____

How is the present earth destroyed? 2 Peter 3:10

Describe the New Jerusalem.
Revelation 21:2_____
Revelation 21:11_____
Revelation 21:12_____
Revelation 21:14_____
Revelation 21:16_____
Revelation 21:21_____
Revelation 21:22_____
Revelation 21:23_____
Revelation 21:24_____
Revelation 21:25_____
Revelation 22:2_____
Revelation 22:5_____

Who will see the faces of God and Christ's? Revelation 22:3-4; 14:1

What mark will they have on their forehead? Revelation 22:4; 14:1

Who will not be allowed to enter the New Jerusalem? Revelation 21:27

LIFE APPLICATION

You have completed the 7,000 year history of mankind from Adam and Eve to the New Heaven, New Earth, and the New Jerusalem. Stand back and see the completed majestic picture of the Bible. Close in prayer thanking God for His wonderful Book, the Bible, and how this study has changed your life.

The BIBLE addresses three groups of people. [1 Corinthians 10:32].

The GENTILES: Genesis 1-11,

ISRAEL: Genesis chapters 12-Revelation [excluding the PAULINE EPISTLES],

and

The CHURCH: Romans-Philemon [PAULINE EPISTLES].

ch. 27
White
Throne of
Judgement
for the
unsaved
(Rev. 20:11-15)

ch.23
Bema
Seat for
the saved
(I Cor. 3:12-15)

ch.22
Rapture
of the
Church
(I Thess. 4:17)

Church (present)
Unprophesied
MYSTERY

ch. 20

chs. 21, 22

CHURCH

ch. 26, 27

ch. 24,25

Great Tribulation
(Matt. 24:21)

Man's sin
(II Tim. 3:1-7)

God's command
The grace of God
(Eph. 2:11-22)
Eph.3:1-9)

KINGDOM

Kingdom
established
(Matt. 25:34, Rev. 20:4)

Kingdom
Proclaimed
(Matt. 24:14)

7 years   1,000 years

Lake
of
Fire
Rev.
20:15

Revelation

GRACE
about 2,000 years

Philemon
Titus
1 & 2 Timothy
1 & 2 Thessalonians
Colossians
Philippians
Ephesians
Galatians
1 & 2 Corinthians
Romans

ADAM	NOAH	ABRAHAM	MOSES	DAVID	JESUS
ch. 1	Chapters of the A Puzzle with Three Pieces (text)	ch. 2	chs. 3 - 7	chs. 8 - 15	ch. 16-19

ch.
16-
19

Man's sin
(Matt. 27:34-42)

LAW

Kingdom
Proclaimed
(Matt. 3:2, 4:23)

Kingdom
Prophesied
(II Samuel 7:12-16)

God's
com-
mand
Mosaic
Law
given

God's
promise
Start of Is-
rael
as a nation
(Gen. 12:1-4)

Kingdom
Postponed
(Rom. 11:11,25)

30
yrs

Acts   Hebrews-Jude

John
Luke
Mark
Matthew

through

about 2,000 years

Exodus

God's
command
(Gen. 9:1)

Man's
sin
(Gen. 11:4)

Genesis

God's
com-
mand
(Gen. 2:17)

Man's
Sin
(Gen. 3:5-7)

about 2,000 years

CHAPTER 1: ORIGINAL CREATION

Read: Genesis 1:1. What did God create?
The Heavens and the Earth

Read: Genesis 1:2. What was "dark and void"?
The Earth

Did God create the heavens and earth "dark and void"? Isaiah 45:18
No

HOW SIN ENTERED THE UNIVERSE

Who was the anointed cherub? Isaiah 14:12
Star of the Morning

Describe the anointed cherub. Ezekiel 28:12-15; Isaiah 14:11,13-14
   A. Every Precious Stone Was His Covering
   B. He Guarded the Mountain of God
   C. He Was Blameless
   D. Pomp
   E. Played the Harp

What job did the anointed cherub have? Ezekiel 28:14
Covering

How did Lucifer sin? Isaiah 14:13-14; Ezekiel 28:15-17
   A. Pride
   B. Wanted to Be like God
   C. Filled with Violence

Where was Lucifer cast after he sinned? Ezekiel 28:17
To the Ground

Who else was thrown to earth? Revelation 12:9
Angels Who Followed Satan

Lucifer's name was changed to what? Revelation 12:9
  A. **The Great Dragon**
  B. **Serpent**
  C. **Devil**
  D. **Satan**

What did the fallen angels become? Luke 4:33-36
  Demons

Where did Satan later appear? Ezekiel 28:13
  Eden

Who observed Satan falling from heaven? Luke 10:18
  Jesus Christ

How does Satan appear today? 2 Corinthians 11:13-14
  As an Angel of Light

What is another name for Satan? Revelation 9:11
  Destroyer

What did Satan destroy? Genesis 1:2
  The Earth

RESTORATION OF THE EARTH

How did God judge this chaotic time? 2 Peter 3:5-6
  God Flooded the Earth

How did God prepare the earth for the habitation of man? Psalm 104:30
  God Renewed the Face of the Ground

On the first day, what did God create? Genesis 1:3-5
  Light and Darkness

On the second day, what did God create? Genesis 1:6-8
  Firmament to Separate Waters

On the third day, what did God create? Genesis 1:9-13
  Sea and Land Divided & Earth Sprouted Vegetation

On the fourth day, what did God create? Genesis 1:14-19
  Moon and Stars for Lights and Seasons

On the fifth day, what did God create? Genesis 1:20-23
   Birds and Fish

On the sixth day, what did God create? Genesis 1:24-31
   Animals and Man

On the seventh day, what did God do? Genesis 2:1-3
   God Rested

How long were the creative days? Genesis 1:8,13,19 .
   Day and Night Was One 24-Hour Day

How did God create the universe and the earth? Hebrews 11:3
   Out of Nothing

THE ATTRIBUTES OF GOD

God is **Spirit**. Read: John 4:24

God is **Infinite**. He is so big He cannot be measured. 1 Kings 8:27; Jeremiah 23:24

God is **Eternal**. He has no beginning and He will never end. Psalm 90:2

God is **Sovereign**. What does that mean? 1 Chronicles 29:11; Daniel 4:35
   He Controls Everything

God Is **All-knowing**. Isaiah 46:10; Psalm 147:5

How powerful is God? Job 42:2
   God does not **Change**. Malachi 3:6
   God is **Good**. Psalm 106:1
   God is **Holy**. He is sinless, pure. Psalm 99:9
   God is **Love**. 1 John 4:8
   God is **Truth**. What He says will happen. John 17:17
   God is **Righteous**. He judges in holiness. Jeremiah 12:1
   God is **Wisdom**. His way is best. Daniel 2:20
   God is **Faithful**. He always keeps His word. 2 Thessalonians 3:3
   God is **Majestic**. He is great and mighty. Psalm 104:1
   God is **Merciful**. He is compassionate and holds back punishment. James 5:11

GOD, A TRINITY

Who are the three persons of God? 1 Thessalonians 1:3-5
   A. God the Father
   B. God the Son
   C. God the Holy Spirit

MAN, A TRINITY

How did God make man? Genesis 1:26
   In His Own Image

What did God breathe into Adam? Genesis 2:7
   Breath of Life

Name the three parts of man. 1 Thessalonians 5:23
   A.   Spirit
   B.   Soul
   C.   Body

How was Eve made? Genesis 2:21-23
   From Adam's Rib

Where did Adam and Eve live? Genesis 2:15
   Garden of Eden

What did God want Adam and Eve to do? Genesis 1:26
   Rule the Animals

HOW SIN ENTERED THE HUMAN RACE & GOD'S COMMANDS

What command did God give to Adam and Eve? Genesis 2:17
   Eat from All Trees Except the Tree of Knowledge of Good and Evil

What other commands did God give Adam? Genesis 1:28; 2:15
   A. Fill the Earth
   B. Cultivate and Keep the Garden

What did God tell Adam to eat? Genesis 1:29-30
   Fruits and Vegetables

What punishment would be applied for disobeying? Genesis 2:17
   Death

Who tempted Eve? Genesis 3:1
Serpent

Who was the serpent? Revelation 12:9
Satan

How was Eve tempted? Genesis 3:2-5
With The Forbidden Fruit

What lie did Satan tell Eve? Genesis 3:4
You Will Not Die

How did Satan attempt to make God look bad? Genesis 3:5
Satan Wanted It to Appear That God Was Withholding Something Good

How did Satan appeal to Eve? Genesis 3:6
A. Through Her Eyes (Fruit Looked Good)
B. Pride (Would Make Her Like God)
C. Her Mind

How does Satan cause you to doubt?
The Same Way

What lies does Satan want you to believe about God?
That He Can't Be Trusted

How does he entice you through your senses?
Lust

What are the steps that lead to sin? James 1:14-15
A. Feeling of Desire Leads to Lust
B. Lust Acts
C. Sin Accomplished

What should you do when you are tempted? 2 Corinthians 10:5
Don't Let Your Thoughts and Feelings Go Unchecked, Take Your Thoughts and Feelings Captive, Obey Christ

When Adam ate the forbidden fruit, was he deceived? 1 Timothy 2:14-15
No

MAN'S DISOBEDIENCE

When did Adam and Eve die spiritually? Romans 5:17
>   **When They Ate the Forbidden Fruit**

How did Adam and Eve's sin affect all mankind? Romans 5:12
>   **Their Sin Spread to All Men**

What happened to Adam and Eve? Genesis 3:23-24
>   **They Were Thrown Out of the Garden of Eden**

SIN BRINGS JUDGMENT

How did God punish the MAN? Genesis 3:17-19
>   **Man Would Have to Work Hard**

How did God punish WOMAN? Genesis 3:16
>   **A. Pain at Childbirth**
>   **B. Husband to Rule over the Wife**

How did God punish the EARTH? Genesis 3:17-18
>   **Thorns and Thistles**

How did God punish the SERPENT? Genesis 3:14-15
>   **A. To Crawl on His Stomach**
>   **B. Enmity Between Satan and the Seed of the Woman**

How did Adam and Eve die years later? Genesis 5:5
>   **Physically**

ANIMAL SACRIFICES INSTITUTED

Why was atonement between God and man needed?
>   **A. All Humanity Has Sinned. Romans 5:12**
>   **B. Sin Separates Man from a Holy God. Romans 3:23**
>   **C. Man Is Unable to Pay for His Sin. Romans 6:23**

LIFE APPLICATION

Who was the seed of the woman? Matthew 1:21
>   **Christ**

Who was the seed of the serpent? Revelation 13:1,2
>   **The Great Beast Also Called the Antichrist.**

How did Satan bruise Christ? 1 Corinthians 2:8
    Crucified the Lord Jesus

How did Christ's death on the Cross crush Satan's dominion and headship? Revelation 1:17-18
    Christ Has the Keys of Death & Hell

Name the first two children of Adam and Eve. Genesis 4:1-2
    A. Cain
    B. Abel

Who did Eve think Cain was? Genesis 4:1
    The Man Child, or Man, the Lord

Who did Eve think was the Man, the Lord? Genesis 3:15
    The Promised Messiah

What offering did Cain give to the Lord? Genesis 4:3
    Fruit

What offering did Abel bring? Genesis 4:4
    The Lamb

What did Abel's sacrifice show? Hebrews 11:4
    A. Believed God
    B. He Was Righteous

Why didn't God accept Cain's offering? Hebrews 9:22
    The Sacrifice Had No Blood

Which attributes of God were evident in God's dealing with Cain in Genesis 4:6-7?
    All Knowing
    Holy
    Love
    Wisdom
    Merciful

Why did Cain kill Abel? Genesis 4:4-5
    Cain Was Jealous Because Abel's Sacrifice Was Accepted and His Was Not

Why would Satan want Abel dead? Genesis 3:15
    The Savior Was to Come Through Abel's Lineage

How did God punish Cain? Genesis 4:13-14
  A. The Earth Wouldn't Yield for Him
  B. Vagrant and Wanderer
  C. Sent Away From the Presence of God

What did Cain leave? Genesis 4:16
  The Presence of the Lord

What did God do for Adam and Eve? Genesis 4:25
  God Gave Them Another Son - Seth

Who was Seth's son? Genesis 4:26
  Enosh

What did the family of Seth begin to do? Genesis 4:26
  Call on the Name of the Lord

Why is it important to know the genealogy of Adam? Luke 3:23,36-38
  It Is the Genealogy of Jesus Christ

Name 5 things the family of Cain started.
  Genesis 4:17 Building
  Genesis 4:19 Polygamy
  Genesis 4:20 Cattle Raising
  Genesis 4:21 Music
  Genesis 4:22 Manufacturing

Why was God sorry He made man? Genesis 6:4-5
  A. Giants Resulted from Intermarriage with Fallen Angels
  B. Corrupted Humanity

Who were these fallen angels? Jude 6-7
  Angels Who Did Not Keep Their First Estate

What did the fallen angels do? Genesis 6:2,4
  They Took Human Wives

What did this union produce? Genesis 6:4
  Giants

What happened to these fallen angels? 2 Peter 2:4-5
  God Put Them in Pits of Darkness Awaiting Judgment

Why would Satan want the human race corrupted? Genesis 3:15
So the Promised Messiah Would Not Come

Why did Noah and his family find favor with God? Genesis 6:9
A. They Were Righteous
B. They Didn't Intermarry with Fallen Angels

Why did God decide to destroy all mankind and animals? Genesis 6:12,17
Mankind and Animals Had Corrupted Their Way

What did God tell Noah to build? Genesis 6:14
An Ark

What was to go in the ark? Genesis 7:2-3
A. Male and Female of Each Species of Animal
B. 7 of Each Animal for Clean Sacrifice
C. Birds, Male and Female

While Noah was preparing the ark, what did he do? 2 Peter 2:5
He Was a Preacher of Righteousness

What would come after Methuselah's death? Genesis 6:17
A Flood of Water

How long did Methuselah live? Genesis 5:27
969 Years

How big was the ark?   Genesis 6:15
300 Cubits

How long did it take Noah to build the ark? Genesis 6:3
120 Years

Who was preserved through the flood? Genesis 7:13
Noah, Ham, Shem, and Japheth, and Their Wives

Who closed the door after all were aboard the ark? Genesis 7:16
The Lord

Until this time, how was the earth watered? Genesis 2:6
By a Mist

How long did Noah and his family wait before it began to rain? Genesis 7:10
7 Days

From where did the flood waters come? Genesis 7:11
Underground Rivers and Rain

How high did the flood waters rise? Genesis 7:20
15 Cubits Higher than the Highest Mountain

What was the outcome of the flood? Genesis 7:21
All Flesh Died

What did Noah do after he left the ark? Genesis 8:20
Sacrificed Animals and Worshiped God

GOD'S NEW COMMANDS

What did God command Noah? Genesis 9:1,7
Multiply and Fill the Earth

How many times did God command to "fill the earth"? Genesis 9:1,7
Two

What was the significance of the repetition of the command?
It Was a Strong Command

How do we know that the principles of Human Government are still in effect today in the Church?
Romans 13:1-2
We Are Told to Obey Governing Authorities

When city, state, or national laws are disobeyed, who is being opposed? Romans 13:3-4
God

Why are laws necessary in a nation? Romans 13:4
So People Will Do What Is Good

What other commands did God give Noah?
Genesis 9:2:   **Man Given Dominion over the Animals**
Genesis 9:3-4:   **Animals Could Be Eaten in Addition to Fruits and Vegetables**
Genesis 9:5-6:   **Capital Punishment Was Established (A Life for Life)**
How did God show that He would never again destroy the earth with water? Genesis 9:13-16
He Put a Rainbow in the Sky

In the future, how will God destroy the earth? 2 Peter 3:10
Fire

Read: Genesis 9:24-27. Name the three prophecies that Noah gave for his sons.

Canaan, Ham's Son Was Cursed and Would Serve the Other Two

Shem Would Have Canaan as His Servant

Japheth would dwell in the Tents of Shem and Would Be Served by Canaan

What purpose would the descendants of Japheth have?

Nations Were to Be Enlarged Through Japheth, Who Was to Experience Shem's Spiritual Blessing.

What purpose would the descendants of Shem have? Genesis 9:26

Shem Would Be Spiritually Blessed

What purpose would the descendants of Ham have? Genesis 9:25

To Be a Servant People

Who was Canaan? Genesis 10:6

The Son of Ham or Noah's Grandson

HISTORY

TOWER OF BABEL

What does God declare is the only way for us to get to Him? John 14:6; Titus 3:5-7

Through Christ

Why did the people build the Tower of Babel? Genesis 11:4

To Get to Heaven by Their Own Effort

What was Satan attempting to destroy?

Their Faith and Obedience to a Living God

In Genesis 11:3-4, the people said "Let us." What did they demonstrate?

Self Will Over God's Will, They Refused to Scatter

How was this the same as Lucifer's and Adam and Eve's sin? Isaiah 13:14

Lucifer, Adam and Eve Wanted Their Own Way

How did God punish this sin? Genesis 11:9

He Confused the Languages

Who is the "Us" in Genesis 11:7? See Genesis 1:26

God the Trinity, Plural One

How did the nations begin? Acts 17:26
God Established Boundaries and Areas of Nations

SIN BRINGS JUDGMENT

What does this tell you about God's purposes? Isaiah 46:9-10
God's Plans and Purposes Will Never Be Thwarted

CHAPTER 2: NATION OF ISRAEL BEGAN

From what nation did Abram come? Genesis 11:31
Abram Was a Gentile from Ur of the Chaldees

The book of Genesis is called the Patriarchal, Father, Age. Who controlled the family, including married children? Genesis 11:31
The Father

Who served as a military leader? Genesis 14:14-15 (318 soldiers)
The Father

Who represented his family before God? Genesis 12:1-3
The Father

How did the father serve as the priest for his family? Genesis 15:9-10; 8:20
The Father Offered the Sacrifice

God changed Abram's name to **Abraham**. Genesis 17:5

God changed Sarai's name to **Sarah**. Genesis 17:15

How was Abraham made righteous before God? Genesis 15:6
He Believed God

How was Abraham's faith perfected before God? James 2:21-22
He Offered up Isaac

What were Abraham and his descendants to observe forever? Genesis 17:10
Circumcision

What was Israel's seal of righteousness? Romans 4:11
Circumcision

Why was Abraham blessed? Genesis 22:18
> **Because He Obeyed God**

GOD'S COMMAND (PROMISE)

What did God promise Abram if he would leave his country and family? Genesis 12:1-3
> **Land**

Genesis 12:2
> **A. A Great Nation**
> **B. Bless Him**
> **C. Make His Name Great**
> **D. Be a Blessing**

Genesis 12:3
> **A. Bless Them That Bless Abraham**
> **B. Curse Them Who Curse Abraham**
> **C. Through Abraham All Families of the Earth Would Be Blessed**

Why did God want Abram to leave his father? Joshua 24:2
> **Terah Was an Idolater**

Abraham took Hagar, Sarah's servant, and she bore Abraham a son. What was his name?
Genesis 16:3,11
> **Ishmael**

How old was Abram when Ishmael was born? Genesis 16:16
> **86**

How many sons did Ishmael have? Genesis 17:20
> **12**

Who did they become? Genesis 25:16
> **12 Tribes of the Gentiles**

HISTORY

Isaac was the promised son God gave to Abraham and Sarah. How old was Abraham when Isaac
was born? Genesis 21:5
> **100 Years Old**

What did God command Abraham to do? Genesis 12:1
> **Leave His Father and Relatives**

How did Abraham disobey God? Genesis 11:31-32

He Took His Father and His Nephew, Lot

The name "Isaac" means laughter. Why was Abraham's son named laughter?
Genesis 17:17; 18:11-12.

Because Abraham and Sarah Both Laughed When God Said They Would Have a Son

What promise did God make to Abraham? Genesis 17:19

God's Covenant Was an Everlasting Covenant

Name the sons of Isaac. Genesis 25:26

Esau and Jacob

The name "Jacob" means deceptive. What new name did God later give to Jacob? Genesis 32:28

Israel

How did Jacob obtain his birthright and blessing? Genesis 25:27-34

By Deception

Why did Jacob regard his birthright in this way? Hebrews 12:16

He Was a Profane Man

How did Esau regard his birthright? Genesis 25:34

He Hated It

Name Jacob's sons through Leah, his wife. Genesis 35:23

Reuben, Simeon, Levi, Judah, Issachar, Zebulun

Name Jacob's sons through Leah's servant girl, Zilpah. Genesis 35:26

Gad, Asher

Name Jacob's sons through Rachel. Genesis 35:25

Joseph, Benjamin

Name Jacob's sons through Rachel's servant, Bilhah. Genesis 35:25

Dan, Naphtali

From which son of Jacob was Messiah, Jesus Christ, to come? Genesis 49:10

Judah

Who is Shiloh? Isaiah 9:6

"Shiloh" Means Peace and Christ Is the Prince of Peace.

Who was Jacob's favorite son? Genesis 37:3
Joseph

Why did Joseph's brothers hate him? Genesis 37:3
Joseph's Father Gave Him a Coat of Many Colors

Why else did his brothers hate him? Genesis 37:4-8
Joseph's Dreams Showed That He Would Rule over Them

What did Joseph's brothers do to get rid of him? Genesis 37:23-24
They Put Joseph in a Pit

How did Joseph get to Egypt? Genesis 37:28
His Brothers Sold Him to Midianites.

How did Joseph obtain power and position in Egypt? Genesis 41:15-33
He Interpreted Pharaoh's Dream

What did Joseph become in Egypt? Genesis 41:40-44
Second in Command

Whom did Joseph marry? Genesis 41:45
Asenath

How old was Joseph when he became ruler in Egypt? Genesis 41:46
30

Name Joseph's sons. Genesis 41:51-52
Manasseh and Ephraim

Why did Joseph's brothers and their families move to Egypt? Genesis 43:1-2
Famine

What did Joseph tell his brothers about their selling him into slavery? Genesis 45:5
A. Don't Feel Guilty for Selling Me
B. God Used it to Provide Food for Them

How did Joseph regard his brothers' sin against him? Genesis 50:20
That They Meant it for Evil, but God Used it for Good

How many of Jacob's family settled in Egypt? Genesis 46:27
70

CHAPTER 3: ISRAEL CAPTIVE IN EGYPT

After the Hyksos kings were dethroned, who came to power? Exodus 1:8
A King Who Didn't Know Joseph

Why was this new pharaoh afraid of the Israelites? Exodus 1:9-10
The Israelites Outnumbered the Egyptians

What did this pharaoh king do to the Israelites? Exodus 1:11
Enslaved Them

Even before Israel was a nation, what did God prophesy about Israel? Genesis 15:13
That Israel Would Be Enslaved for 400 Years

What training did Moses receive in Egypt? Acts 7:22
He Was Educated in All the Learning of the Egyptians

Who wrote the first five books of the Bible called the Pentateuch? Exodus 24:4
Moses

What are the names of Moses' parents? Exodus 6:20
Amram and Jochebed

What did pharaoh command concerning Israelite male infants? Exodus 1:16
That They Be Killed

How did Moses' mother save his life? Exodus 2:1-3
She Put Moses into a Basket a and Set It in the Reeds of the River

Who found baby Moses? Exodus 2:5
Pharaoh's Daughter

What did Pharaoh's daughter do with the baby? Exodus 2:9; Acts 7:21
Hired Moses' Mother to Nurse Him

What did Pharaoh's daughter name the baby? Exodus 2:10
Moses

How long did Moses live in the palace in Egypt? Acts 7:22-23
40 Years

Why did Moses flee from Egypt? Acts 7:24-29
He Killed an Egyptian

Did the Israelites understand that Moses was to be their leader? Acts 7:24-25
> **No**

To what country did Moses flee? Exodus 2:15
> **The Land of Midian**

How long was Moses in Midian as a shepherd? Acts 7:30
> **40 Years**

Whom did Moses marry? Exodus 2:21; Numbers 12:1-2
> **Zipporah**

Name Moses' two sons. Exodus 18:3-4
> **Gershom and Eliezer**

Why was God seeking to kill Moses' firstborn son? Exodus 4:23-25
> **Moses Had Not Circumcised His Sons**

Moses, on the eve of delivering Israel, was reminded that without circumcision the Israelites were cut off from the covenant. Why? Genesis 17:10
> **Because It Was a Sign of Obedience to the Covenant**

What was Israel's seal of righteousness? Romans 4:11
> **Circumcision**

Why did the Israelites cry out to God? Exodus 2:23
> **Because They Were Enslaved**

How did God respond to their cry? Exodus 2:24
> **God Remembered His Covenant to Abraham**

Who commissioned Moses to be the leader of the Israelites? Exodus 3:1-6;10-12
> **God**

What did God send to enable the Israelites to leave Egypt? Exodus 7:4
> **God Sent Judgments**

What was the first plague? Exodus 7:19-20
> **Water to Blood**

What did the magicians in Egypt do? Exodus 7:22
> **Magicians Duplicated That Miracle**

What was the second plague? Exodus 8:6
    Frogs

What did the magicians do? Exodus 8:7
    Magicians Duplicated That Miracle

What was the third plague? Exodus 8:17
    Lice

Could the magicians duplicate this miracle? Exodus 8:18
    No

What was the fourth plague? Exodus 8:21
    Flies

How did God protect the Israelites? Exodus 8:22
    the Israelites Were Not Plagued with Flies

What was the fifth plague? Exodus 9:6
    Livestock Died

How did God protect Israel? Exodus 9:6
    None of Israel's Livestock Died

What was the sixth plague? Exodus 9:9
    Boils

How did the boils affect the magicians? Exodus 9:11
    Magicians Were Plagued with Boils

What was the seventh plague? Exodus 9:25
    Hail

How did God protect the Israelites? Exodus 9:26
    Israelites Were Not Destroyed by Hail

What was the eighth plague? Exodus 10:14-15
    Locusts

What was the ninth plague? Exodus 10:22
    Darkness

What was the tenth plague? Exodus 11:5
    Death of Firstborn

How did God protect the Israelites? Exodus 12:22-24
Blood on Door Posts - No One Died

How did Israel commemorate their deliverance from Egypt? Exodus 12:14,24
Feast of Passover

What did the Egyptians give the Israelites as they were leaving Egypt? Exodus 12:35-36
Articles of Clothing, Silver And Gold

How long did it take for the Israelites to travel to Mt. Sinai? Exodus 19:1
3 Months

CHAPTER 4: THE LAW GIVEN TO ISRAEL

GOD'S COMMAND, THE CONDITIONAL MOSAIC LAW SYSTEM

How long were the Israelites at Mt. Sinai? Numbers 10:11
2 Years, 2 Months & 20 Days

What was Israel to be? Exodus 19:6
A Kingdom of Priests, a Holy Nation

To whom was the Mosaic Law given? Romans 9:4
Israelites

What did Israel say? Exodus 19:8
They Would Do All That God Said

Why was the Law given? Romans 3:19-20
A. **All the World Would Be Accountable to God**
B. **Knowledge of Sin**

What are the 3 parts of the Law?
A. **Commandments. Read: Exodus 20. These Were the Moral Laws, the Ten Commandments.**
B. **Judgments. Read Exodus 21-23. These Were Laws Concerning the Social Life of Israel.**
C. **Ordinances. Read: Exodus 24-40. These Were Laws Concerning the Religious Life of Israel.**

Why was the Law called a CONDITIONAL covenant? Exodus 19:5
To Be God's People, They Had to Fulfill It

TABERNACLE

What did God tell Moses to erect? Exodus 25:9
The Tabernacle

How did Moses know how to build the tabernacle? Hebrews 8:5
God Showed Moses the Heavenly Tabernacle

Where is the true tabernacle which God made? Hebrews 8:1-2,5
In the Heavens

Where did Jesus go after He made atonement for sin on the Cross? Hebrews 9:11-12
The Perfect Tabernacle in the Heavens

What is the Lord Jesus Christ doing in the Heavenly Tabernacle? Hebrews 8:1-2
A. High Priest
B. Ministers in the Tabernacle

How did the craftsmen know how to build the tabernacle furniture? Exodus 31:1-3
God Filled the Craftsmen with the Holy Spirit

Before the tabernacle was erected, who served as the priest and offered the animal sacrifices?
Genesis 8:20
Fathers

Who were chosen to be the priests in the tabernacle? Exodus 28:1,41
Aaron and His Sons

Who are Gershom, Merari, and Kohath? Numbers 3:17
Sons of Levi

How were the needs of the priesthood met? Numbers 18:21
The Tithe from Israel Was Given to Them

What was the tithe? Leviticus 27:32
10% of Fruits and Herds

What else was given to the Levites? Leviticus 7:34; Numbers 18:21
Peace Offerings

Who filled the tabernacle after it was completed? Exodus 40:33-34
God

How did Israel know when to begin their journeys? Exodus 40:36
> **The Glory Cloud of God Was Moved Up**

GOD'S DWELLING PLACES

Where did God dwell during Israel's wilderness wanderings? Exodus 40:34
> **The Tabernacle**

Where did God dwell during Solomon's day? 2 Chronicles 7:1
> **Solomon's Temple**

Where did God dwell during Jesus Christ's day? Colossians 2:9
> **In Christ**

Where does God dwell today? 1 Corinthians 6:19
> **In Believers**

SABBATH

To whom was the Sabbath given? Exodus 31:13,16
> **Israel**

What happened to an Israelite who worked on the Sabbath? Exodus 31:15
> **Killed**

When did the early church meet to worship? Acts 20:7; 1 Corinthians 16:2
> **The First Day of the Week**

Why do we worship the Lord on Sunday, the first day of the week? John 20:1-2
> **It Was the Day That Christ Resurrected from the Dead**

FEASTS

The Feast of Passover

How long did the Passover Feast last? Leviticus 23:5-6
> **1 Day**

Why did Israel celebrate this feast? Exodus 12:27
> **To Thank God for the Deliverance from Egypt**

The Feast of Unleavened Bread

Why did Israel celebrate this feast? Exodus 12:27
As a Symbol of the Removal of Corruption and Sin

How long did the unleavened bread feast last? Leviticus 23:5-6
7 days

The Feast of Firstfruits

Why did Israel celebrate the Feast of Firstfruits? Exodus 34:22
To Thank God for the First Fruit of Harvest

What day was Firstfruits celebrated? Leviticus 23:10-11
The Day After the Sabbath

The Feast of Pentecost

What was Israel to celebrate? Exodus 23:16
The End of the Harvest

The Feast of Atonement Leviticus 23:26-32; 16:34

What were the people of Israel not supposed to do on this day?
Work

What were they supposed to do?
Humble Themselves

How long did the feast last?
1 Day

The Feast of the Booths or Tabernacles

How would Israel celebrate the Feast of Tabernacles? Leviticus 23:34,41-43
For 7 Days They Live in Booths

The Feast of Purim

Why did Israel celebrate the Feast of Purim? Esther 9:26-28
To Celebrate Israel's Deliverance Because of Esther

On what feast did Jesus die? John 19:14
Passover

On what feast did Jesus rise from the dead? 1 Corinthians 15:20
> **Feast of Firstfruits**

On what feast did Jesus send Israel the prophesied Holy Spirit to prepare them for the harvest?
Acts 2:1
> **Feast of Pentecost**

ANIMAL SACRIFICES

Why were animals sacrificed? Hebrews 9:22
> **Without Shedding of Blood There Is No Forgiveness**

How did animal sacrifices picture the work of the Lord Jesus in the future? John 1:29
> **Blood from Animals Only Covered Sin but the Blood of the Lord Jesus, the Lamb of God, Takes Away Sin.**

Why did priests continually offer sacrifices? Hebrews 10:3-4
> A. **Reminder of Sin**
> B. **The Blood of Animals Could Not Remove Sin**

What did the death of Christ accomplish? Hebrews 9:12
> **Eternal Redemption**

Why are animal sacrifices no longer needed? Hebrews 10:10,12
> **Christ's Death Was a Once for All Sacrifice**

The ____offering was offered for sin and defilement. Leviticus 6:25
> **Sin**

Why was the trespass offering made? Leviticus 6:1-6,25
> A. **Unfaithfulness to the Lord in Deception**
> B. **Robbery**
> C. **Lied**
> D. **Sworn Falsely**
> E. **Sin and Defilement**

What offering was given as a voluntary act of worship? Leviticus 3:1
> **Peace Offering**

How long was this offering to be made unto the Lord? Leviticus 3:17
> **Forever**

What offering showed Israel's gratitude for God's provision? Leviticus 2:1-3
> **Grain Offering**

Read: 2 Corinthians 5:21. Tell how Jesus Christ was our substitute.

He Made Him to Be Sin for Us

LIFE APPLICATION

What did Jesus take of ours?

Our Sin

When we trust Him as our Savior, what does He give to us?

His Righteousness

DIETARY CHANGES

To whom were these new dietary laws given? Leviticus 11:2

Israel

Where does the term "clean" animals first appear? Genesis 7:1-2

Noah Took "Clean" Animals onto the Ark

What was the purpose of the "clean" animals? Genesis 8:20

Clean Animals Were Used for Sacrifice and Burnt Offerings

What two characteristics had to be present before an Israelite was permitted to eat an animal? Leviticus 11:3-4

A. Must Have a Divided Hoof
B. Must Chew the Cud

Name two characteristics of the edible fish. Leviticus 11:12

A. Must Have Fins
B. Scales

What type of birds could Israel not eat? Leviticus 11:13-19

Meat Eating Birds

Name two characteristics of edible insects. Leviticus 11:20-21

A. Must Walk on All Four Legs
B. Must Have a Jointed Leg to Jump

God wanted the nation of Israel to be "clean." Why? Isaiah 60:1-3

To Be an Example to the Nations

What can be eaten today in the Church? 1 Timothy 4:4

Everything That Is Good

Why are we to pray and thank God for our food? 1 Timothy 4:5
So Our Food Is Sanctified

Does God put conditions on what we can eat today? 1 Timothy 4:4
No, but We Are to Eat It with Thanksgiving

BAPTISMS

Where does the word "wash" first appear in the Bible? Exodus 29:4
The Priests Were to Be Baptized to Consecrate Them for Service

What was the purpose of baptism? Numbers 19:9
Purification From Sin

What nation was given water baptism as a perpetual statute? Numbers 19:9-10
Israel

How were Gentiles (foreigners) received into the camp? Numbers 31:19,23
Purified by Baptism for Impurity

How were the priests cleansed? Exodus 30:18-20
Baptized

If the priests were not baptized, what happened to them? Exodus 30:21
They Would Die

How was the baptism for purification from sin performed?
Numbers 19:5   Sacrifice - a Heifer Was Burned
Numbers 19:17   Ashes Put into Vessel and Water Added
Numbers 19:18   A Hyssop Bush Was Dipped into Water. The Unclean Person
                            Was Sprinkled (Baptized) With the Water.

How long were "baptisms" (washings) to continue? Hebrews 9:10-12
Until Christ Died on the Cross and Shed His Blood

Why were washings (baptisms) only needed until Christ? Hebrews 9:12
Christ's Blood Provides Eternal Forgiveness of Sin

After Christ offered a "once for all sacrifice for sin" what did He do? Hebrews 10:12
He Sat down at the Right Hand of God

As God used water baptism to cleanse Israel of sin, how is our sin forgiven today in the Church?
Romans 5:9; 3:24-25
By the Shed Blood of Jesus Christ on the Cross

In the future Davidic Kingdom for Israel, how will God forgive sin and impurity? Zechariah 13:1
A Fountain for Sin and Impurity

What did Paul say about water baptism? 1 Corinthians 1:17
Christ Did Not Send Him to Baptize

Why was Paul glad he only baptized a few people? 1 Corinthians 1:17
So the Cross of Christ Should Not Be Made Void

JOHN'S BAPTISM FOR FORGIVENESS OF SIN - (WATER)
Mark 1:4-6; Matthew 21:23-25; John 3:22-23; 4:1; John 10:37-42; Mark 11:29-33;
Luke 3:1-22; Luke 7:24-39; Luke 20:1-8; John 1:15-33; and Acts 1:22

Who is doing the baptizing?
John

Who is baptized?
Israel

Why?
For the Forgiveness of Sin

JESUS' BAPTISM TO FULFILL ALL RIGHTEOUSNESS - (WATER)
Matthew 3:13-15

Who is doing the baptizing?
John

Who is baptized?
Jesus

Why?
To Fulfill All Righteousness

CHRIST BAPTIZING WITH THE HOLY SPIRIT - (NOT WATER)
John 1:33; Acts 2:3-4; Luke 3:16; Matthew 3:11-16; Mark 1:8; Acts 1:3-5; and 11:15-16

Who is doing the baptizing?
Christ

Who is baptized?
Believing Israel

Why?

To Receive Power

PENTECOSTAL BAPTISM - (WATER and a MIRACLE FOLLOWED
Acts 2:38; 8:12-18; 8:35-39; 9:18-19; 16:14-15; 19:1-8; 22:12-16; Mark 16:14-19; Matthew 28:19; and 1 Corinthians 1:14-17

Who is doing the baptizing?

Peter

Who is baptized?

Believing Israel

Why?

So They Could Receive Forgiveness of Sin And The Holy Spirit

DEATH BAPTISM - (NOT WATER)
Mark 10:8; Luke 12:49-51

Who is doing the baptizing?

Death

Who is baptized?

Christ

Why?

For Sin

BAPTISM FOR THE DEAD - (NOT WATER)
1 Corinthians 15:29

Who is doing the baptizing?

Martyrdom

Who is baptized?

Believers

Why?

They Were Faithful to the Lord

THE TYPE BAPTISM OF NOAH'S ARK - (NOT WATER)
1 Peter 3:18-21

Who is doing the baptizing?
The Flood

Who is baptized?
Noah and his family

Why?
They were saved through the flood

BAPTISM OF FIRE - (NOT WATER)
Luke 3:16; Matthew 3:11

Who is doing the baptizing?
Christ

Who is baptized?
Israel

Why?
Judgment

MOSES' BAPTISM - (NOT WATER)
1 Corinthians 10:2

Who is doing the baptizing?
God

Who is baptized?
Israel

Why?
To Identify Israel With Moses

TRADITIONAL JEWISH BAPTISMAL CEREMONIES - (WATER)
Luke 11:38; Mark 7:1-8

Who is doing the baptizing?
Individuals

Who is baptized?
Hands

Why?
Ceremonial Cleansing

TRADITIONAL JEWISH BAPTISMS - (WATER)
Hebrews 6:1-3; 9:10

Who is doing the baptizing?
Individuals

Who is baptized?
Israel

Why?
Cleansing of Sin

HOLY SPIRIT BAPTIZING BELIEVERS INTO THE BODY OF CHRIST - NOT WATER
1 Corinthians 12:12-14; Romans 6:3,4; Galatians 3:25-29; Ephesians 4:1-4; Colossians 2:9-15

Who is doing the baptizing?
Holy Spirit

Who is baptized?
Believers

Why?
A Seal of Salvation Putting Believers into the Church, the Body of Christ

CHAPTER 5: ISRAEL WANDERED IN THE WILDERNESS

When Israel left Mt. Sinai, which tribe led the march? Numbers 10:14
Judah

Where did Israel go after they left Mt. Sinai? Deuteronomy 1:19
Kadesh-Barnea

How long was Israel at Kadesh? Deuteronomy 1:46
Many Days

What did God tell Moses to do? Numbers 13:1-2
Send 12 Spies to Spy out Canaan

After the twelve spies returned, what did the ten spies report? Numbers 13:31
They Gave a Bad Report of Giants in the Land

Joshua and Caleb, the other two spies, gave good reports. What did Joshua and Caleb report?
Numbers 14:7-9
They Reported that the Land Was Good & God Would Give Them Victory Over Giants

How did Israel respond? Numbers 14:10
Israel Wanted to Stone Joshua and Caleb

What happened to Israel because of unbelief? Numbers 14:33-34
They Were to Wander in the Desert for 40 Years

While Israel wandered in the wilderness, which gods did they worship? Acts 7:41-43
Hosts of Heaven, Molech, Star of Remphan, Human Sacrifices

Why didn't God permit Moses to go into the Promised Land of Canaan? Numbers 20:8-12
Disobedience: Moses Hit the Rock Instead of Speaking to It

How did this show that the Law was conditional?
If You Obeyed You Were Blessed, If You Disobeyed You Were Not Blessed.

Who was the rock? 1 Corinthians 10:4
Christ

How did Moses see the Promised Land? Deuteronomy 32:49
He Viewed it from Mt. Nebo

Describe Moses' physical condition before he died. Deuteronomy 34:7
Strong Body and Eyes

What happened to Moses on the mountain? Deuteronomy 34:1,5
He Died

After Moses' death, where did he go? Deuteronomy 32:50
He Was Gathered to His People

Who succeeded Moses as leader of Israel? Numbers 27:22-23
Joshua

What was God's opinion of Moses? Deuteronomy 34:10
There Was No One like Him - Moses Saw God Face to Face

CHAPTER 6: ISRAEL CONQUERED THE PROMISED LAND

What did God promise Israel? Joshua 1:6
> **Possession of the Land**

How would Joshua have success? Joshua 1:7
> **By Obeying the Law of Moses**

What miracle did God show Israel? Joshua 3:15-17
> **The Jordan River Was Dried up and Israel Went Through on Dry Ground**

How did Israel show they believed God and were ready to enter the land? Joshua 5:5
> **They Circumcised Their Sons**

Why was circumcision important? Genesis 17:10
> **Circumcision Was a Sign of the Abrahamic Covenant**

Name the first city that the Israelites conquered. Joshua 2:1
> **Jericho**

How many spies did Joshua send into the city of Jericho? Joshua 2:1
> **2**

What woman hid the spies? Joshua 2:1,6
> **Rahab**

How did Rahab show she trusted the Lord? Joshua 2:8-11
> **Rahab Believed That God Did the Miracles**

What agreement did Rahab make with the spies? Joshua 2:14
> **To Protect Her Family When Israel Conquered Jericho**

How did the spies escape from Jericho? Joshua 2:15-16
> **Rahab Let Them Down a Rope**

When the Israelites invaded Jericho, how did they know Rahab's home? Joshua 2:18,21
> **A Scarlet Rope in Her Window**

How did the Israelites conquer Jericho? Joshua 6:3
> **By Obeying God**

How did God reward Rahab? Matthew 1:5
> **She Is in the Genealogy of Christ**

How many nations did Israel conquer? Acts 13:18-19
7

How many years did it take to conquer Canaan? Acts 13:20
450

What was God's promise to Israel? Joshua 1:3
Every Place on Which the Sole of Your Foot Treads

What method was used to divide the land? Joshua 18:8-10
Casting of Lots

What was given to the Levites? Joshua 21:1-2
Cities

How many cities were given to Kohath and his family? Joshua 21:4-5
13

How many cities were given to Gershon and his family? Joshua 21:6
13

How many cities were given to Merari and his family? Joshua 21:7
12

What were the "cities of refuge?" Joshua 20:2-3
Places of Safety for People Who Unintentionally Killed Someone

Joshua was ready to die. Name three ways Joshua encouraged Israel.
A. Joshua 23:6   **Obey the Law of Moses**
B. Joshua 23:7   **Don't Worship the Gods of the Surrounding Nations**
C. Joshua 24:19   **Serve the Lord**

Where did Joshua write his book? Joshua 24:26
In the Book of the Law

Before Joshua died, what did Israel promise Joshua? Joshua 24:24
They Would Be Faithful to the Lord

CHAPTER 7: ISRAEL EXPERIENCED CYCLES

Why didn't Israel obey God after Joshua died? Judges 2:10
The Children Were Not Taught about the Lord and How He Helped Israel

What did the new generation do since they did not know about God? Judges 2:11-13
Served Baal and Astarte

How did God feel? Judges 2:14
Angry

How did God punish Israel? Judges 3:8
God Gave Israel into Bondage to Mesopotamia

How many years were the Israelites in bondage to Mesopotamia? Judges 3:8
8

Thee deliverers were called? Judges 2:18
Judges

Who was the first judge of Israel? Judges 3:9
Othniel

How did God empower Othniel? Judges 3:10
The Holy Spirit Came Upon Him

After Othniel led Israel to victory, how long did Israel experience rest? Judges 3:11
40 Years

How long did the judges serve as leaders of Israel? Acts 13:20
Until Samuel, the Prophet

At the end of the book of Judges, what was Israel's condition? Judges 21:25
Lawless

CHAPTER 8: ISRAEL WANTED A KING

What vow did Hannah make to the Lord? 1 Samuel 1:11
If God Gave Her a Son, She Would Give Him Back to the Lord

Who was Hannah's son? 1 Samuel 1:20
Samuel

How did Hannah keep her vow? 1 Samuel 1:24-25
Samuel Went to Live at the House of the Lord and He Served with Eli, the Priest

How did Israel know Samuel was a prophet? 1 Samuel 3:19-20
All of His Prophecies Came True

Why did Israel have victory over the Philistines? 1 Samuel 7:3-4
Idols Were Destroyed. Israel Wanted to Serve the Lord Only.

Why did Israel want a king? 1 Samuel 8:5
Israel Wanted to Be like Other Nations

Who was Israel rejecting? 1 Samuel 8:7
God as Their King

Who was the FIRST king of Israel? 1 Samuel 9:17
Saul

What were Saul's human qualifications to be king? 1 Samuel 9:2
A. Handsome
B. A Head Taller than the Other Israelites

How long did Saul rule? Acts 13:21
40 Years

How did God empower Saul? 1 Samuel 10:10
The Holy Spirit Came upon Saul

List 3 reasons why God rejected King Saul.?
A.   1 Samuel 13:9   Saul Offered a Burnt Sacrifice
B.   1 Samuel 15:17-19   Incomplete Obedience
C.   1 Samuel 28:7-8   Saul Inquired of a Witch

Who only was to offer animal sacrifices? Leviticus 1:17
The Priests

Who succeeded Saul as the SECOND king of Israel? 2 Samuel 5:4
David

How did God empower David to be the King of Israel? 1 Samuel 16:13
The Holy Spirit Came upon David

How long did he reign? 2 Samuel 5:4
40 Years

Name the THIRD king of Israel. 1 Kings 2:12
Solomon

What promise did God make to Solomon? 1 Kings 9:5
God Would Establish His Throne

How did God exalt Solomon? 1 Chronicles 29:25
Giving Him Majesty Never Seen Before

What did Solomon do for the Lord? 1 Kings 6:1
Built the House of the Lord (Temple)

What happened after the temple was completed? 2 Chronicles 7:1-2
The Glory of the Lord Filled the Temple

How many years did Solomon reign over Israel? 1 Kings 11:42
40 Years

What was the extent of Solomon's kingdom? 2 Chronicles 9:26
From the Euphrates River to Egypt

Name Solomon's sins. 1 Kings 11:5-7
- A. **He Worshiped the Goddess Ashtoreth**
- B. **Solomon Did Not Fully Follow the Lord**
- C. **He Built a Place the Idol Chemosh**

How did God punish Solomon's sin? 1 Kings 11:11-12
God Took the Kingdom Away from Solomon During His Son, Rehoboam's, Reign

THE HOLY SPIRIT IN THE OLD TESTAMENT

How did certain Israelites know how to sew the priest's clothing? Exodus 28:3
The Holy Spirit Gave Them Wisdom

Why was Bezaleel given the Holy Spirit? Exodus 31:3-5
- A. **To Give Him Wisdom**
- B. **Understanding**
- C. **Knowledge of All Kinds of Craftsmanship**

What men received the Holy Spirit and why? Numbers 11:16-17
The Elders, to Help with the Work

When did Othniel receive the Holy Spirit and why? Judges 3:9-10
When He Became a Judge So He Could Deliver Israel From Bondage

When did Saul receive the Holy Spirit and why? 1 Samuel 9:17; 10:9-11
When He Was to Be King, This Enabled Him to Do the Job

When did David receive the Holy Spirit? 1 Samuel 16:13
When Samuel Anointed Him to Be King

What happened to King Saul? 1 Samuel 16:14
Because of His Sin, the Holy Spirit Left King Saul and an Evil Spirit Terrorized Him

Why did David receive the Holy Spirit? 1 Samuel 16:1
To Enable Him to Serve as King

Why did King Saul consult the witch of Endor? 1 Samuel 28:15
God Stopped Answering His Prayers

What did Samuel say would happen to King Saul the next day? 1 Samuel 28:19-20
Saul and His Sons Would Die

Where would Saul be after his death? 1 Samuel 28:19
With Samuel

What did King David pray after he sinned with Bathsheba and why? Psalm 51:11
"Do Not Take Your Holy Spirit From Me."

WHAT IS THE DAVIDIC KINGDOM?

What did David want to build for God? 1 Chronicles 28:2
A Temple

Why would God not allow David to build the temple? 1 Chronicles 28:3
David Shed Much Blood

Instead, what did God promise to build for David? 2 Samuel 7:12-13
God Built David a House

How long would the throne of David last? 2 Samuel 7:13,16
Forever

The prophets confirmed that Messiah would come through whose line? Jeremiah 23:5
David's

Who was related to King David? Matthew 1:1
Jesus Christ

Who was born to sit on David's throne? Luke 1:31-32
Jesus Christ

In the Kingdom, over whom will Jesus Christ reign? Daniel 7:14,27
All Peoples and Nations

After Jesus' baptism, what message did He proclaim? Matthew 4:17,23
> **The Gospel of the Kingdom**

CHARACTERISTICS OF THE KINGDOM

What will be the extent of Christ's Kingdom? Zechariah 14:9
> **The Whole Earth**

In what city will Christ's throne be? Zechariah 14:16-17
> **Jerusalem**

In the Kingdom there will be no **War**. Micah 4:3

In the Kingdom there will be no **Hunger**. Amos 9:13-14

In the Kingdom there will be no **Illness**. Isaiah 33:24

In the Kingdom, animals will be **Tamed**. Isaiah 65:25

In the Kingdom, there will be _____. Isaiah 65:20
> **Long Life.**

What will not be in the Kingdom? Isaiah 32:17
> **Infant Mortality**

How will Israel dwell in the Kingdom? Isaiah 32:18
> **Peacefully and Secure**

What is the length of the Kingdom on earth? Revelation 20:6-7
> **1000 YEARS**

CHAPTER 9: ISRAEL WAS DIVIDED

Name the fourth king of Israel. 2 Chronicles 9:31
> **Rehoboam, Solomon's Son**

How long did Rehoboam reign in Jerusalem? 2 Chronicles 12:13
> **17 Years**

What grievous thing did King Rehoboam and Israel do? 2 Chronicles 12:1
> **He Forsook the Lord**

What prophecy was being fulfilled? 1 Kings 11:11-12
> **Because of Solomon's Sin, the Kingdom Was Being Taken Away from Rehoboam**

What did God tell Jeroboam through Ahijah the prophet? 1 Kings 11:30-31
> **Jeroboam Would Rule 10 of 12 Tribes of Israel**

Who tried to put Jeroboam to death? 1 Kings 11:40
> **Solomon**

How did Rehoboam treat Israel harshly? 1 Kings 12:13-15
> **He Made Their Yoke Heavier**

Israel rebelled against Rehoboam. Whom did Israel kill? 1 Kings 12:18
> **Adoram, Because Israelites Did Not Want to Be in Forced Labor**

Who became the king of Israel, the ten tribes? 1 Kings 12:20
> **Jeroboam**

Who was the king of Judah? 1 Kings 12:23; 2 Chronicles 12:13
> **Rehoboam**

HISTORY

There were continual **Wars** between Israel and Judah.

What evil things did Israel, the ten tribes do? 2 Kings 17:16-17
> **A. Served Baal**
> **B. Human Sacrifice**

What happened to Israel because of their sin? 2 Kings 17:22-23
> **Israel Was Carried Away into Exile**

What was Judah's sin? 1 Kings 14:22-24
> **A. They Built a Place to Worship the Asherot**
> **B. Male Cult Prostitutes**

What nation took Judah captive? 2 Kings 24:12
> **Babylon**

Who was the king of Babylon? 2 Kings 24:11
> **Nebuchadnezzar**

What else did Babylon carry away? 2 Kings 24:13-14
>   A. **Treasures**
>   B. **Men of Valor**

What did Nebuchadnezzar and his army do to the temple? 2 Kings 25:8-9
>   **Burned It with Fire**

What was done to the walls around the temple? 2 Kings 25:10
>   **They Were Broken Down**

What country took Israel into captivity? 2 Kings 17:23
>   **Assyria**

HISTORY - MAJOR AND MINOR PROPHETS

How does the Bible warn unsaved people of danger? John 3:36
>   **Warns That the Wrath of God Will Abide on Them.**

What danger does the Bible warn Christians to avoid? Ephesians 4:17-24
>   **Don't Sin like Unsaved People**

How are unsaved people captive? Ephesians 2:1-3
>   **To Satan, the Prince and Power of the Air**

What does God want for Christians? Galatians 5:1
>   A.   **To Stand Firm in God's Word**
>   B.   **Stay Free of Anything That Enslaves**

CHAPTER 10: ISRAEL REBUILT THE TEMPLE

What did Cyrus decide to do? Ezra 6:3
>   **Gave Permission to Rebuild the Temple**

Who was to go to Jerusalem? Ezra 1:5
>   **Heads of Judah and Benjamin, the Priests and the Levites**

How did Judah get money to rebuild the temple? Ezra 1:4
>   **Freewill Offering Taken**

What man led the first company of Jews? Ezra 2:1-2
>   **Zerubbabel**

What was the first thing to be rebuilt? Ezra 3:2-3
The Altar

What did Israel do? Ezra 3:3
Offered a Burnt Offering

What did Israel celebrate? Ezra 3:4
Feast of Tabernacles (or Booths)

What was built the second year? Ezra 6:15
The Temple

What man led the second company of Jews back to Jerusalem? Ezra 7:6
Ezra

What did Ezra do in Jerusalem? Ezra 7:10
A.   **Studied the Law**
B.   **Protected the Law**
C.   **Taught the Statutes and Ordinances to Israel**

What caused a revival? Ezra 10:1-3
A. **Reading Scripture**
B. **Prayer and Confession**
C. **People Repented**

Who led the third company of Jews back to Jerusalem? Nehemiah 1:1; 2:5
Nehemiah

What did the third company accomplish? Nehemiah 2:17; 7:1
Rebuilt the Wall

LIFE APPLICATION

What does the last book of the Old Testament prophesy? Malachi 3:1
A.   **A Messenger to Come**
B.   **To Clear the Way for Christ's Coming**

When Messiah came, what was to happen to Israel? Malachi 3:2-3
They Were to Be Purified

How were these prophecies fulfilled? Mark 1:2-4
John the Baptist Was the Messenger and Announced the Lord's Appearance

How was Israel purified of their sin? Mark 1:4-5
> **Israel Was Baptized for the Forgiveness of Sin**

CHAPTER 12: JESUS, KING OF THE JEWS, WAS BORN

JESUS CHRIST, HIS HUMANITY

Why does Matthew begin his book giving the genealogy of Jesus Christ? Matthew 1:1
> **To Show Christ Was Related to King David and Abraham**

An angel appeared to Mary. What did he tell her? Luke 1:31
> **She Would Have a Son**

Why did Mary think this was strange? Luke 1:27,34
> **She Was a Virgin**

Who was the father of her child? Luke 1:35
> **God**

What did the angel tell Mary to name the child? Luke 1:31
> **Jesus**

How did Mary respond? Luke 1:38
> **"I'm Willing"**

What would this child do? Luke 1:32-33
> A. **He Would Be Great**
> B. **He Would Sit on the Throne of David**
> C. **He Would Reign Over the House of Jacob Forever**
> D. **His Kingdom Would Never End**

How did Mary regard Jesus? Luke 1:47
> **God, Her Savior**

When Joseph learned Mary was with child, what did he do? Matthew 1:19
> **He Wanted to Put Her Away Secretly**

What did the angel of the Lord tell Joseph? Matthew 1:20
> **Don't Be Afraid to Wed Mary**

Whom did Mary visit? Luke 1:39-40
> **Zacharias and Elizabeth**

How long did Mary stay with Elizabeth? Luke 1:56
3 Months

Why did Mary and Joseph go to Bethlehem? Luke 2:4-5
To Register

Under what time was Jesus born? Galatians 4:4
Law

Who came to see Jesus, the King of the Jews? Matthew 2:1-2
The Magi

Who was Jesus? Luke 2:2
King of the Jews

Where did the Magi locate the young Child? Matthew 2:11
In the House

Name two things the Magi did. Matthew 2:11
A. Worshiped
B. Gave Gifts

Why did the Magi bring gifts? Matthew 2:2
Jesus Christ Was a King

Why didn't the Magi return to King Herod? Matthew 2:12
God Warned Them

An angel appeared to Joseph. What did the angel tell him? Matthew 2:13
Take Mary and Flee to Egypt

What did King Herod do to the children of Bethlehem? Matthew 2:16
They Were Killed

How did God provide for Mary and Joseph's needs in Egypt? Matthew 2:11
The Gifts Which the Magi Had Given Them

How did Mary and Joseph know when to return to Nazareth? Matthew 2:19-20
An Angel Told Them

How long was Mary a virgin? Matthew 1:25
Until after Jesus Was Born

Name the other children that Mary and Joseph had. Matthew 13:55-56; Mark 6:3
James, Joseph, Simon, Judas, Besides Sisters

Whom did Jesus say was to be honored? Luke 11:27-28
Those Who Obeyed the Word of God

How old was Jesus when he went to Jerusalem with Mary and Joseph? Luke 2:42
12

Why did they go to Jerusalem? Luke 2:41
To Observe the Feast of Passover

Why did John the Baptist baptize Israel? Mark 1:4-5; Matthew 3:6; Luke 3:3
For the Forgiveness of Sin

Second Corinthians 5:21 says that Jesus had no sin. Why did He allow Himself to be baptized by John? Matthew 3:15; John 1:31
A. To Fulfill All the Righteousness of the Law
B. To Be Presented to Israel

How did Christ take away the Law? Colossians 2:14
He Fulfilled It and Nailed It to His Cross

As the forerunner of Jesus Christ, what did John the Baptist preach? Matthew 3:2
"Repent, for the Kingdom of Heaven Is at Hand"

CHAPTER 13: JESUS CHRIST, THE KING, PROCLAIMED THE KINGDOM TO ISRAEL

JESUS CHRIST, HIS MESSAGE

What gospel did Jesus teach? Matthew 4:23
The Gospel of The Kingdom (Jesus Preached That the Kingdom Was at Hand. Matthew 4:17)

Jesus preached that the Kingdom was _____ _____. Matthew 4:17
At Hand

What does the term "at hand" mean?
Ready to Begin (Greek indicates meaning of nearby)

Where does the term "kingdom of heaven" originate? Daniel 7:27
Kingdoms Under the Whole Heaven

Who was to reign over all the "kingdoms under the whole heaven"? Daniel 7:13-14
The Son of Man

Who was the Son of Man? Luke 9:22
Jesus Christ

What signs accompanied the message of the gospel of the Kingdom? Matthew 4:23
Healing

Why did Jesus heal? Isaiah 35:5-6
Because in the Kingdom There Would Be No Sickness

What authority would the apostles have in the Kingdom? Matthew 19:28
They Would Sit on 12 Thrones Ruling the 12 Tribes of Israel

Jesus sent the twelve apostles to _____ only. Matthew 10:6
Israel

What message did Jesus tell the apostles to proclaim? Matthew 10:7
The Gospel of the Kingdom

What was the inheritance of believing Israel? Matthew 5:5
The Earth

In the Lord's prayer, Jesus told His disciples to pray for the Kingdom to come to _____,
Earth

Where was the Kingdom prophesied to be established? Zechariah 14:9
Over the Whole Earth

In the Kingdom there would be no what? Isaiah 2:4
War

How did Jesus show His deity and power?   Matthew 8:24-26
He Calmed the Storm

What miracle did Jesus perform and why? Matthew 9:23-25
He Brought a Dead Girl Back to Life

What would be long in the Kingdom? Isaiah 65:20
Life

What gospel did Jesus continue to teach? Matthew 9:35
Gospel of the Kingdom

Why did Jesus teach in parables? Matthew 13:10-11
    So Believing Israel Would Know the Secrets (Mysteries) of the Kingdom

What miracle did Jesus perform in Matthew 14:18-21 and why?
    He Fed 5000 People

According to Amos 9:13-14 what would there be in the Kingdom?
    Gardens and Vineyards

QUALIFICATIONS FOR ISRAEL TO ENTER THE KINGDOM

What did believing Israel do with their money to show that they were indeed disciples of Jesus?
    A. Matthew 10:9   **Sold All, Gave to the Poor**
    B. Luke 12:33   **In the Kingdom, They Would Be Given 100 Times What They gave Away**

Why? Mark 10:29-30
    It Was Their Reward for Giving up All of Their Possessions

How was believing Israel to abase themselves?
    Matthew 18:3-4   **They Came to Jesus as a Child**
    Matthew 23:12   **Humbled Themselves**
    Matthew 16:24   **Denied Themselves**
    Mark 9:35   **Chose to Be Last**

What were the qualifications for eternal life in the Kingdom?
    Mark 10:29-30   **Leave Family, Sell All**
    Matthew 19:16-17   **Keep the Commandments**
    James 2:24   **Faith That Was Perfected by Works**

What happened to believing Israel if they didn't maintain good works?
    Matthew 5:22,28-29   **Went to Hell**
    Matthew 18:8-9,33-35   **Hell**
    John 5:29   **Resurrection of Judgment**

What did Jesus tell believing Israel about bearing fruit?
    Matthew 7:19-21   **Bear Fruit or Be Thrown into the Fire**
    John 15:5-6   **Anyone Not Bearing Fruit Was Thrown into the Fire**

LIFE APPLICATION

In our daily lives, how are we helped by knowing Israel's history? Romans 15:4
    It Is for Our Instruction to Give Perseverance, Encouragement, and Hope

The Kingdom on earth was planned by God **Since** the foundation of the world. Matthew 13:35

The church was planned by God from **Before** the foundation of the world. Ephesians 1:4

CHURCHES

What did Jesus give Peter? Matthew 16:19
> **Keys to the Kingdom**

These keys were to the _____ church. Matthew 16:19
> **Kingdom of Heaven**

What could be forgiven using the power of the keys? John 20:23; Matthew 16:19
> **Sins**

When did Peter use this authority? Acts 5:2-5,8-9
> **Ananias & Sapphira Lied, Peter Knew and Judged Their Sin**

Why did Jesus pronounce "woes" on the Pharisees? Matthew 23:27-28
> **They Appeared to Be Righteous but They Were Lawless**

Why did Jesus weep over Jerusalem? Matthew 23:37
> **Because of Their Sin of Unbelief; He Was Their King, but as a Nation, Israel Rejected Him**

Where will Jesus' throne be in the Kingdom?   Isaiah 24:23
> **Jerusalem**

What did the apostles ask Jesus? Matthew 24:3
> **When Would He Come and When Would the End of the World Occur**

What was to be the next age to come? Matthew 24:21
> **The Great Tribulation**

What are some of the characteristics of the Great Tribulation? Matthew 24:5-7,12,15-16
> A.   **Wars**
> B.   **Famines**
> C.   **Earthquakes**

What people will preach the gospel of the Kingdom during the Great Tribulation? Revelation 7:4
> **Sons of Israel**

To whom will the gospel of the Kingdom be preached? Matthew 24:14
> **The Whole World**

After the Great Tribulation, what will occur? Matthew 24:29-30
>   A.   **Signs in Heaven**
>   B.   **Son of Man (Christ) Appearing in Power and Glory**

Who are taken away in judgment? Matthew 24:39
>   **The Unbelieving**

What does Christ do? Matthew 25:31-32
>   **He Comes in Glory and Sits on His Glorious Throne**

Who is at Christ's right hand? Matthew 25:33
>   **The Sheep**

What does Christ say to Israel, the sheep? Matthew 25:34
>   **"Come, You Are Blessed, Inherit The Kingdom"**

GOSPELS

Jesus preached the gospel of the **Kingdom.** Matthew 4:23

What gospel told of the Old Testament and New Testament saints? Romans 1:1-4
>   **Gospel of God**

What gospel makes Jesus the object of faith? 2 Corinthians 2:12
>   **The Gospel of Christ**

What gospel is an aspect of both the Kingdom and Body of Christ? Ephesians 6:15
>   **Gospel of Peace**

What gospel did Paul preach? Acts 20:24
>   **The Grace of God**

Paul referred to the gospel of grace as _____ gospel. Romans 16:25
>   **My**

The gospel that was preached to Israel was called the gospel of _____. Galatians 2:7
>   **Circumcision**

The gospel that is to be preached to the Church, the body Christ is called the gospel of the
_____. Galatians 2:7
>   **Uncircumcision**

Which gospel is to be proclaimed today during the Church, the Body of Christ? Acts 20:24; Ephesians 3:1-3

The Gospel of the Grace of God

What warning is given concerning the gospel of the grace of God? Galatians 1:8-9

If Anyone Preaches Anything Else Besides the Gospel of Grace, He Is Accursed

CHAPTER 14: JESUS CHRIST'S RELATIONSHIP TO THE LAW AND ISRAEL

JESUS CHRIST, HIS RELATIONSHIP TO THE LAW

In which time did Jesus live? Galatians 4:4

Law

When Jesus was born, what Mosaic Laws did Mary and Joseph observe? Luke 2:21-24
- **A.** **Circumcision**
- **B.** **Purification**
- **C.** **Offered a Turtle Dove**

Did Jesus teach the necessity of an animal sacrifice? Matthew 5:23

Yes

What did Jesus tell his apostles to obey? Matthew 23:1-2

The Law of Moses

What did Jesus tell the leper? Luke 5:14

Follow the Prescribed Cleansing According to the Law of Moses

What was the weakness of the Mosaic Law? Hebrews 10:4

The Blood of Animals Couldn't Take Away Sin

What was the purpose of the Law? Romans 3:20

To Give the Knowledge of Sin

What did Jesus say about the Law? Matthew 5:17-18

He Came to Fulfill It

When did the Mosaic Law end? Colossians 2:14; Ephesians 2:15-16

At the Cross

JESUS CHRIST, HIS RELATIONSHIP TO ISRAEL

To what nation only did Jesus send the apostles? Matthew 10:6
> **Israel**

To what nations were the apostles not to go? Matthew 10:5
> **Gentiles and Samaritans**

When Jesus and the apostles ministered to Israel, how did God regard the Gentiles? Ephesians 2:12
> **A. Excluded From Israel**
> **B. Strangers of the Covenant of Promise**
> **C. No Hope**
> **D. Without God**

What message did Jesus tell the apostles to proclaim? Matthew 10:7
> **Gospel of the Kingdom**

Why did Jesus and the apostles minister only to Israel? Romans 15:8
> **To Fulfill the Promises to Israel**

A Gentile centurion came to Jesus. What did he ask Jesus? Matthew 8:6
> **For Jesus to Say the Word, and His Servant Would Be Healed**

What did Jesus command for the centurion? Matthew 8:10
> **For His Great Faith**

What did Jesus call the Gentile woman? Mark 7:28
> **A Dog**

What did Jesus do because of her faith? Mark 7:29
> **Healed Her Daughter**

What were the Jews not to do? Matthew 7:6
> **Give Holy Things to the Gentiles**

To what nation were Jesus and the twelve apostles to minister FIRST? Mark 7:27
> **Israel**

To whom was God's salvation offered FIRST? Acts 3:26
> **Israel**

How did God want Gentiles to be saved? Isaiah 60:1-3; Luke 2:30-32
> **Gentiles Were to Come to Israel's Light**

CHAPTER 15: ISRAEL REJECTED JESUS CHRIST AT THE CROSS

JESUS CHRIST, HIS WORK

How did Mary prepare Christ for His death? Matthew 26:7,12
>   **She Put Perfume on Him**

Name two things that Jesus told His apostles would happen. Matthew 26:29,31
>   **A.   The Next Time He Drank the Cup with Them Would Be in the Kingdom**
>   **B.   Fall Away**

Why was Jesus "grieved and distressed"? Matthew 26:38
>   **Because of His Imminent Death**

What did Jesus pray? Matthew 26:39
>   **If Possible, Not to Drink the Cup (Die)**

Describe Jesus' betrayal and capture. Matthew 26:46-50
>   **Judas Led Captors to Jesus, Then Kissed Jesus with a Betrayal Kiss**

Why did He willingly go with the soldiers? Matthew 26:54
>   **So the Scriptures Would Be Fulfilled**

After Jesus was captured, where was He taken? Matthew 26:57
>   **To Caiaphas, the High Priest's House**

What did the disciples do? Matthew 26:56
>   **They All Fled (Fell Away)**

What did the chief priests and Council do to Jesus?
>   **Matthew 26:65 Tore His Clothes Saying Jesus Blasphemed by Saying He Was God**
>   **Matthew 26:67 Spit on Jesus**
>   **Matthew 27:2   Bound Him and Took Him to Pilate**

Who did Jesus say He was? Matthew 27:11
>   **King of the Jews**

How did Israel reject Jesus Christ as their King? Matthew 27:22-23
>   **They Wanted Jesus to Be Crucified**

How did Israel take responsibility for Jesus' death? Matthew 27:25
>   **They Said, "His Blood Be on Us and Our Children."**

Jesus was turned over to be crucified. Describe what the Roman guards did to Him.

> **Matthew 27:28 Stripped Him and Put on a Scarlet Robe**
> **Matthew 27:29 Crown of Thorns**
> **Matthew 27:30 Spit on Him - Beat Him with a Reed**
> **Matthew 27:31 Took Robe Off - Put His Garment On & Led Him Away to Be Crucified**
> **Matthew 27:34 Wine with Gall Offered to Christ**
> **Matthew 27:35 Jesus Was Crucified**

What was written on the sign put over the head of Jesus? Matthew 27:37
> **"This Is Jesus, the King of the Jews"**

When did God forsake His Son, Jesus? Matthew 27:46
> **At the 9th Hour**

Why did God forsake His Son, Jesus? 2 Corinthians 5:21; 1 Peter 2:24
> **Jesus Became Sin for Us**

Was Jesus killed, that is, His life taken from Him? John 10:18, Matthew 27:50
> **No - He Laid His Life Down**

MAN'S DISOBEDIENCE

The New Testament (Covenant) began at the _____. 1 Corinthians 11:25
> **Cross**

What happened to the veil in the Temple when Jesus died? Matthew 27:51
> **The Veil Was Torn from Top to Bottom**

Who requested the body of Jesus? Matthew 27:57-58
> **Joseph of Arimathea**

What did Joseph of Arimathea do with the body of Jesus? Matthew 27:60
> **Put it in a New Tomb**

How did the Romans secure the tomb? Matthew 27:64-66
> **A. Posted Guards**
> **B. Seal upon the Stone**

Why were the Romans afraid? Matthew 27:64
> **That the Followers of Jesus Would Steal Christ's Body**

What happened after three days? Matthew 28:2
> **An Earthquake Occurred & an Angel Rolled Away the Stone**

How did the soldiers act when they saw the angel and empty tomb? Matthew 28:4
They Shook and Were Stiff with Fear

What did the angel tell the women? Matthew 28:6
Jesus Is Risen - Jesus Is Alive

Who saw Christ after He was resurrected from the dead?
1 Corinthians 15:5 Peter & the 12 Apostles
1 Corinthians 15:6 500 People at One Time
1 Corinthians 15:7 A. James B. All the Apostles
1 Corinthians 15:8 Paul
Luke 24:13-15   Two on the Road to Emmaus

Name two reasons why the resurrection of Jesus Christ is so important. 1 Corinthians 15:14
A.   Our Faith Is in Vain If He Didn't Resurrect
B.   We Are Still in Our Sins

Did Satan know what Christ would accomplish through the Cross? 1 Corinthians 2:8
No

GOD'S DUAL PURPOSE IN THE CROSS

To whom was the secret of the Church first revealed? Ephesians 3:8
Paul

LIFE APPLICATION

How do we experience God's grace at salvation? Ephesians 2:8-9
By Faith, Not by Works

How else do believers experience God's grace? Ephesians 1:3
By Being Given Every Spiritual Blessing

CHAPTER 16: THE KINGDOM OFFERED TO ISRAEL

SURVEY OF ACTS

JESUS' COMMANDS TO ISRAEL

After the resurrection, what did Jesus command the eleven Apostles to do? Mark 16:14-20
(1)   **Vs. 15 "Go into All the World and Preach the Gospel."**
(2)   **Vs. 16 "He Who Believes and Is Baptized Shall Be Saved."**
(3)   **Vs. 17 Signs to Follow, Casting out of Demons, Tongues to Follow Belief, and Serpents Couldn't Hurt Believing Israel**

Why was water baptism given to Israel? Mark 1:5; Acts 2:38
> **Cleansing of Sin**

What did the apostles ask the Lord Jesus after the resurrection? Acts 1:6
> **About When the Kingdom Was Coming**

What was Jesus Christ's answer to them? Acts 1:7
> **"It Is Not for You to Know"**

When would Israel receive the Kingdom's "time of refreshing"? Acts 3:19
> **After Israel Repented for Killing Christ**

Where did Jesus Christ tell the apostles to go? Acts 1:4
> **Jerusalem**

What was the Holy Spirit to do? Acts 1:8
> **To Come upon Believing Israel**

What prophecy to Israel was about to be fulfilled? Acts 1:4-5
> **Believing Israel Would Be Baptized with the Holy Spirit**

What happened to the Lord Jesus? Acts 1:11
> **He Ascended**

Where did the Lord Jesus go? Acts 1:11
> **Back to Heaven**

Why did there need to be twelve apostles? Matthew 19:28
> **To Sit on the 12 Thrones Judging the 12 Tribes**

What was still being offered to Israel? Acts 1:6, 3:19-20
>**The Kingdom Was Still Being Proclaimed**

How did the apostles know they were to replace Judas? Acts 1:20
>**It Was Prophesied in Psalms**

What were the two qualifications were needed to be a candidate for apostle? Acts 1:21-22
>A.   **To Have Been with Jesus from His Baptism to His Ascension**
>B.   **Must Have Seen the Resurrection of Christ**

What two men were qualified to be an apostle? Acts 1:23
>A. **Joseph, Called Barsabus**
>B. **Matthias**

What man was chosen? Acts 1:26
>**Matthias**

THE HOLY SPIRIT AT PENTECOST

Was the coming of the Holy Spirit PROPHESIED to Israel? Ezekiel 36:26-27
>**Yes**

What would the Holy Spirit cause Israel to do? Ezekiel 36:27
>**To Walk in God's Ordinance**

What then was Israel to do? Isaiah 60:3
>**Be a Light to the World**

When was the Holy Spirit given to Israel? Acts 2:1-4
>**At Pentecost**

What did Joel's prophecy say about the Holy Spirit? Joel 2:28-29
>**He Would Be Poured out**

What did Joel's prophecy say would follow the outpouring of the Holy Spirit upon Israel?
Joel 2:30-31
>**A Display of Wonders in the Sky and Earth**

 To whose sons and daughters did Joel's prophecy refer? Acts 2:5;14,22,36; 3:12
>**Jews of Peter's day**

How did Peter tell Israel they could receive the Holy Spirit? Acts 2:38
>A.   **Be Baptized for the Forgiveness of Sin**
>B.   **Receive the Holy Spirit**

148

What followed repentance, water baptism, and the gift of the Holy Spirit? Acts 2:43

> **Miracle**

Why did Peter and John go to Samaria? Acts 8:14-17
- A.   **To Pray for Believers**
- B.   **To Give Them the Holy Spirit**

At Samaria, how did the believing Jews receive the Holy Spirit? Acts 8:17

> **By the Laying of the Hands**

Where was the Holy Spirit to come? Acts 8:16

> **Upon Them**

How did Israel as a nation respond to the Holy Spirit? Acts 7:51

> **Israel Rejected God, the Holy Spirit**

COMPARISON STUDY OF THE WORKING OF THE HOLY SPIRIT

ISRAEL IN THE OLD TESTAMENT See Page 35	ISRAEL AT PENTECOST See Page 60	TODAY IN THE CHURCH See Page 80
1)	1)	1)
2)	2)	2)
3)	3)	3)
4)	4)	4)
	5)	5)
	6)	6)
		7)
		8)
		9)
		10)
		11)
		12)

LIFE APPLICATION

Name three reasons why it is important to know how the Holy Spirit works today in the Church, the Body of Christ.
- **1) To Have Assurance of Salvation**
- **2) To Know the Holy Spirit Will Never Leave Us**
- **3) To Know the Ways He Helps Us**

CHAPTER 17: ISRAEL REJECTED GOD, THE HOLY SPIRIT

LAST DAYS OF ISRAEL

What people were in Jerusalem at the feast of Pentecost? Acts 2:5
> **Devout Jews**

What did the Jewish believers in the upper room receive? Acts 2:4
> **A. Holy Spirit**
> **B. Tongues**

What were these tongues? Acts 2:6
> **Human Languages**

Besides Joel's prophecy, where else were tongues prophesied to Israel? 1 Corinthians 14:21
> **In the Mosaic Law**

What were the Jews experiencing? Acts 2:17
> **The Last Days**

Pentecost was the "last days" of what nation? Acts 2:5, 14, 22, 36
> **Israel**

Describe the "last days" of the Church, the Body of Christ. 2 Timothy 3:1-5
> **Lawlessness, Selfish Indulgence, Ungodliness**

What did Peter preach to Israel? Acts 3:14-15,19
> **Israel's Guilt That They Killed Christ**
> **Asked for a Murderer to Be Freed in His Place**

If Israel repented, Who would have returned for Israel? Acts 3:20-21
> **Jesus Christ**

What are the times of refreshing? Acts 1:6
> **The Kingdom**

What did Peter tell Israel to do? Acts 3:19
> **Repent**

How many Jews repented? Acts 2:41; 4:4
> **3,000 & 5,000**

How did the believing Jews try to set up the Kingdom? Acts 4:32
> **By Setting up a Commune and Sharing Equally**

Why were the high priests jealous? Acts 5:16-17
> **Everyone Was Being Healed**

What happened to the apostles? Acts 5:18
> **They Were Put into Jail**

What did Peter say when the leaders commanded him not to preach about Christ? Acts 5:29
> **"We must Obey God and Not Man."**

What did he continue to teach? Acts 5:30-32
> A. **Jesus' Death**
> B. **Jesus' Resurrection**

What did the apostles think of the flogging they received? Acts 5:41
> **They Rejoiced in the Suffering**

Describe Stephen. Acts 6:8
> A. **Full of Grace**
> B. **Had Power**
> C. **Performed Signs and Wonders**

What did Israel do to Stephen as he proclaimed God's faithfulness to Israel? Acts 7:58
> **They Stoned Him**

Who was Israel rejecting? Acts 7:51
> **God the Holy Spirit**

What did Stephen see? Acts 7:56
> **Jesus Christ, Standing at the Right Hand of God**

What did the standing position of God mean? Isaiah 3:13
> **Standing Was the Position Before Judgment Was Executed**

Why did God forgive Israel for their crucifixion of Jesus Christ? Luke 23:34
> **Jesus Prayed for God to Forgive Israel**

Why couldn't God forgive Israel's rejecting the Holy Spirit? Matthew 12:31-32
> **Jesus Prophesied That this Sin Wouldn't Be Forgiven**

How had Israel tasted of the heavenly gift? Acts 2:38
> **Believing Israel Was Given the Holy Spirit**

How had Israel seen the power of the age to come? Acts 2:3-4
> **The Holy Spirit Came upon Them - with Tongues of Fire**

Why couldn't Israel be "renewed to repentance"? Acts 7:51; Matthew 12:31-32
    A. **Israel Rejected the Holy Spirit**
    B. **That Sin Would Not Be Forgiven**

SIN BRINGS JUDGMENT

How long will the partial hardening of Israel continue? Romans 11:25
    ntil the Fullness (Completion) of the Gentiles

How does this hardening affect Israel today? 2 Corinthians 3:15
    A Veil of Darkness Darkens Their Understanding

How did God use Israel's unbelief to benefit everyone? Romans 11:11,15
    Salvation Is Offered to the World

When is this hardness removed from individual Jews? 2 Corinthians 3:16
    When a Jew Comes to Christ, the Veil Is Removed

How will Israel respond when the Gospel of the Kingdom is once again preached during the Great Tribulation? Zechariah 12:10; Romans 11:26
    All of Israel Will Be Saved

CHAPTER 18: SAUL (PAUL) WAS SAVED AND BECAME THE APOSTLE TO THE CHURCH

Describe Saul's background. Philippians 3:4-6
    A Jew of the Tribe of Benjamin, a Hebrew of the Hebrews, a Pharisee & He Kept the Law

Who was in agreement with Stephen's murder? Acts 8:1
    Saul

What did Saul do to believers in Christ? Acts 8:3; 9:1
    Put Christians in Jail & Put Them to Death

Why did Saul want to go to Damascus? Acts 9:2
    To Kill Christians

What happened to Saul on the road to Damascus? Acts 9:4; 22:14
    A Bright Light

Who did Saul see? Acts 22:14
    Jesus Christ

Where did the men take Saul? Acts 9:10-11
Damascus

How did Saul receive the Holy Spirit? Acts 9:17
Laying of the Hands

What miracle followed? Acts 9:18
The Scales Fell from His Eyes

What did Saul do? Acts 22:16
Was Baptized to Wash Away His Sins

To whom did the Lord Jesus send Saul? Acts 9:15
A.   Gentiles
B.   Kings
C.   Sons of Israel

Why couldn't Paul stay in Jerusalem? Acts 9:22-23
The Jews Planned to Kill Him

Where did Paul go? Galatians 1:17
Arabia

How long did Paul stay in Arabia? Galatians 1:18
3 Years

While in Arabia, what did Paul receive? Ephesians 3:6-8
The Message of Grace to the Church That Jew & Gentile Were One Body

Who revealed the secret of the Church, the Body of Christ, to Paul? Galatians 1:12
The Risen Christ

Did Paul receive this new gospel from Peter? Galatians 1:12
No

Who did Paul say he was? 1 Timothy 2:7
A. Preacher
B. Teacher
C. Apostle to the Gentiles

Who commissioned Paul to be an apostle? 2 Timothy 1:1
God

Why was Paul sent to the Gentiles to proclaim the Church? Romans 11:14
    To Provoke Israel to Jealousy

CHAPTER 19: GOD SHOWED ISRAEL THAT THERE WAS NOW NO PARTIALITY BETWEEN THE JEWS AND GENTILES

What did God show to Peter? Acts 10:11-12
    A Sheet Full of Unclean Animals

What did God tell Peter? Acts 10:13
    Kill and Eat

What did Peter answer? Acts 10:14
    These Foods Are Unclean

How many times did God say that the animals were clean? Acts 10:15-16
    3

Why was the command repeated?
    It Was an Important Change of Commands

What did Peter understand? Acts 10:34
    God Now Doesn't Show Partiality Between Peoples

What did God command Peter to do? Acts 10:19-20
    "Go with the Men at Your Home."

Where did Peter go? Acts 10:25
    To Cornelius' Home

Who was Cornelius? Acts 10:22
    A Gentile Centurion

What did Peter preach to Cornelius? Acts 10:34-35,39-40
    A.   **Everyone Is Welcomed to Come to Christ**
    B.   **Christ's Death on the Cross**
    C.   **Christ's Resurrection**

What happened to Cornelius? Acts 10:44,46,48
    A.   **The Holy Spirit Came upon Him**
    B.   **Spoke in Tongues**
    C.   **He Was Baptized**

Why was Peter amazed? Acts 10:45
That the Gift of the Holy Spirit Was Poured out on Gentiles, Too

Why did Paul later accuse Peter of being a hypocrite? Galatians 2:11-13
Because Peter Stopped Associating with Gentiles

LIFE APPLICATION

What is God's plan for Jews and Gentiles today? 2 Corinthians 3:16
That Both Jew and Gentile Will Turn to the Lord for Salvation

How does God see believing Gentiles today? Ephesians 2:19
Gentiles Are No Longer Strangers and Aliens

CHAPTER 20: GOD REVEALED THE MYSTERY OF THE CHURCH, THE BODY OF CHRIST, TO PAUL

PAUL, HIS MESSAGE

After Paul was saved, he went to Arabia. What gospel did he receive there? Ephesians 3:1-7
The Gospel of Grace

Who revealed the secret message of the Mystery, the Church to Paul? Galatians 1:12; 2 Corinthians 12:1
Jesus Christ

When did Paul first see Peter and James? Galatians 1:18
3 Years after He Was Saved

How many years passed until again Paul saw the apostles? Galatians 2:1
14

What did the Jewish brethren want to do to Titus? Galatians 2:3
Circumcise Him

Did Paul submit to their demands? Galatians 2:5-6
No

COMPARISON OF PETER AND PAUL'S MINISTRIES

Peter was an apostle sent to the _____. Galatians 2:8
CIRCUMCISION

Paul was an apostle sent to the _____. Galatians 2:8; Acts 26:16-17
> **GENTILES**

Peter preached the Gospel of the _____ to Israel. Matthew 4:23; 10:7
> **KINGDOM**

Paul preached the gospel of _____. Acts 20:24
> **GRACE**

Since Peter and Paul had different messages and were apostles to different groups of people, what did they decide to do? Galatians 2:9-10
> **A. Peter Would Go to the Circumcision**
> **B. Paul Would Go to the Gentiles**

Where did the apostles and the scattered believing Jews continue to preach? Acts 11:19
> **To the Jews Alone**

Where did Paul preach? Romans 15:20
> **Not Where Peter Had Preached**

Did Peter fully understand the new message of the Church that God revealed to Paul? 2 Peter 3:15-16
> **No**

What does the word "Scripture" mean? 2 Timothy 3:16
> **Words Inspired by God**

How did Peter endorse Paul's writings? 2 Peter 3:16
> **He Mentions Paul's Letters as Scriptures**

PAUL, HIS MINISTRY

Who accompanied Paul on his first missionary trip? Acts 13:2
> **Barnabas**

Where did Paul and Barnabas go? Acts 13:4-5
> **Selucia, Cyprus & Salamis**

What people did Paul and Barnabas attempt to reach with the gospel? Acts 13:5
> **The Jews**

What did Paul preach to the Jews? Acts 13:39,43
> **A. Freedom from the Law of Moses**
> **B. Grace of God**

When the Jews refused to believe, to what people did Paul go? Acts 13:46
The Gentiles

What happened to Elymas? Acts 13:8-11
He Was Blinded for a Season

How was this a parallel to what happened to Israel? Compare Acts 13:8-11and Romans 11:10-11, 25
Israel, Because of Unbelief, Was Blinded for a Season

Name the kings to whom Paul preached. Acts 24:3; 25:1; 26:1
  A.   **Felix**
  B.   **Festus**
  C.   **Agrippa**

Israel continued in unbelief. To what people only did God finally send Paul? Acts 26:16-18; 28:28
The Gentiles

Paul went on three missionary trips. How many people did he reach with the gospel of the Grace of God? Colossians 1:23
Every Person under Heaven

Why were the miracles, sign gifts, tongues, and wonders evident during the early ministry of Paul?
1 Corinthians 1:22; 2 Corinthians 12:12
  A. **Jews Required a Sign**
  B. **They Were Signs to Prove Paul Was an Apostle**

LIFE APPLICATION

Where are we to build our foundation today? 1 Corinthians 3:10
On the Foundation Which Paul Laid

What else does the apostle Paul say? 1 Corinthians 11:1; 4:16
To Follow Paul as He Followed Christ

Paul built his foundation on _____. 1 Corinthians 3:11
Jesus Christ

What will believers receive by building on the Church foundation? 1 Corinthians 3:12-14.
A Reward

Name the elementary teachings of Christ.
- A.   **Repentance**
- B.   **Dead Works**
- C.   **Washings**
- D.   **Laying on of Hands**
- E.   **Resurrection of the Dead**
- F.   **Eternal Judgment**

In what books do you read about the elementary teachings of Jesus?
   Matthew, Mark, Luke, and John

CHAPTER 21: TODAY, THE CHURCH, THE BODY OF CHRIST

To whom did God first reveal the Mystery of the Church, the Body of Christ? Ephesians 3:3-7; Colossians 1:25-26
   Paul

What was Paul's greatest desire? Ephesians 3:10
   To Make The Church Known

How do believers get into the Church, the Body of Christ? Ephesians 1:13; 1 Corinthians 12:12-13
- A.   **Hear the Gospel of Salvation**
- B.   **The Holy Spirit Baptizes the Believer into the Church**

Who is the Head of the Church? Ephesians 1:22-23; Ephesians 5:23
   Christ

Does Israel have any national priority? 1 Corinthians 12:13; Galatians 3:28
   No

How does God see believers today? Galatians 3:26
   As Sons of God

How and why does God want us to respond to others? Romans 15:7
   We Are to Accept Other Unconditionally as Christ Unconditionally Accepts Us

What is salvation by? Ephesians 2:8-9
   Grace through Faith Alone

What does God want us to do after salvation? Ephesians 2:10
   Good Works

What are we to do with the gospel of grace? 2 Corinthians 5:20
Beseech Others to Be Reconciled to God

Why is it important for us to be ambassadors for Christ? 1 Corinthians 3:13-14
Obedience to Christ and to Receive a Reward

SPIRITUAL BLESSINGS

In Christ, believers are unconditionally...

forgiven of all **SIN**. Colossians 2:13
ACCEPTED in the Beloved.   Ephesians 1:6 (KJV)
COMPLETE in Him. Colossians 2:10
given an **INHERITANCE**, Ephesians 1:18
made **SONS** of God. Ephesians 1:5
made **SAINTS.** Ephesians 1:1
given His **LOVE** in our hearts. Romans 5:5
given a **PURPOSE** for living. Romans 8:28-29; 2 Corinthians 4:15-18
are **BAPTIZED** into the Body of Christ. 1 Corinthians 12:12-13
there are no **DISTINCTIONS** in the Church. Galatians 3:28
are made new **CREATION**. 2 Corinthians 5:17
given the Holy Spirit as a **SEAL**. Ephesians 1:13-14
indwelt by the Holy Spirit until the day of **REDEMPTION**. 1 Corinthians 6:19;
    Ephesians 4:30
given power in the **INNER** man by the Holy Spirit. 2 Corinthians 4:7; Ephesians 3:16
have victory over **SIN**.   Romans 6:14
given a **GIFT** to serve the Lord. Romans 12:6
have victory over **DEATH**. 2 Corinthians 5:8-9
given **ETERNAL** life, Romans 6:23
are given God's never-ending **LOVE.** Romans 8:39
have **THE HOLY SPIRIT** to understand the Bible. 1 Corinthians 2:12-15

THE HOLY SPIRIT IN THE CHURCH

How and when is the Holy Spirit received? Ephesians 1:13-14
The Gospel Is Heard, Believed and the Holy Spirit Is Given upon Belief

Is any other work (something we do) required? Romans 4:5; Ephesians 2:8-9; Titus 3:5-6; 2
Timothy 1:9
No, Not of Works

Why is the Holy Spirit given to believers? 2 Corinthians 5:5
As a Pledge

What relationship do believers have with God? Romans 8:15-16
Children of God

Where does the Holy Spirit place believers? 1 Corinthians 12:13
Into the Church, the Body of Christ

This union makes the believer a member of what church? 1 Corinthians 12:27
His Body

Name four ways the indwelling Holy Spirit helps us. 2 Corinthians 4:7
- A.   **Gives Power**
- B   **Victory over Sin**
- C   **Helps Us Understand the Bible**
- D   **Gives Love**

Over what does the Holy Spirit give us power?

Romans 6:6	**Old Self**
1 Corinthians 2:12-13	**Spirit of the World**
Romans 5:5	**Disappointment**

How are we to be led in the Christian life? Romans 8:14
By the Holy Spirit

How do we know we are walking in the Spirit? Ephesians 5:9-11
- A.   **We Try to Please the Lord in All We Do and Say**
- B.   **Reprove the Works of Darkness (Sin)**

What fruit will be evident in our lives when the Holy Spirit is at work in us? Galatians 5:22-23
- A. **Love**
- B. **Joy**
- C. **Peace**
- D. **Patience**
- E. **Kindness**
- F. **Goodness**
- G. **Faithfulness**
- H. **Gentleness**
- I. **Self-control**

How does the Holy Spirit help you study the Bible? John 14:26
- A. **Will Teach Us All Things**
- B. **Call Things to Remembrance**

The Holy Spirit doesn't bring attention to Himself. Who does the Holy Spirit glorify? John 16:14
Jesus Christ

When do we experience the power of the Holy Spirit? 2 Corinthians 12:9
When We Are Weak

What did Paul say about his weaknesses? 2 Corinthians 12:9
He Welcomed Weaknesses So He Could Experience Christ's Power

How does the Holy Spirit help us when we pray? Romans 8:26-27
A. He Intercedes for Us
B. Answers Are According to God's Will

What does God accomplish with the various circumstances and trials in our lives? Romans 8:28-29
A. Works it for Good
B. So We Will Be Conformed to the Image of Jesus Christ

What does the Holy Spirit give believers? Ephesians 4:8
Gifts

Does everyone have the same gifts? Romans 12:6
No

What is the purpose of these gifts? Ephesians 4:12
Equipping the Saints for the Work of the Ministry

What does a fleshly life do to the Holy Spirit? Ephesians 4:30; 1 Thessalonians 5:19
Grieves and Quenches

Describe believers' lives when they are not obeying the Lord. 1 Corinthians 3:3
Fleshly

How does God want believers to be? Ephesians 5:1-2
A.   Believers of God
B.   Walk in Love
C.   Serve Others

How can believers know they are walking in the Spirit?

Ephesians 4:24	**Holy**
Ephesians 4:25	**Speak Truth to all**
Ephesians 4:26-27	**Forgive Others Unconditionally**
Ephesians 4:28	**Don't Steal - Be Honest**
Ephesians 4:29	**Don't Curse**
Ephesians 4:31	**Put Away Anger**
Ephesians 4:32	**Be Kind**
Ephesians 4:15	**Speak the Truth in Love**

How does Satan appear? 2 Corinthians 11:14

As an Angel of Light

Is our warfare against people? Ephesians 6:12

No, Against Spiritual Forces of Darkness

Where does warfare against Satan occur? 2 Corinthians 10:5

In Our Minds

What is the goal for believers? 2 Corinthians 10:5

To Bring Our Thinking into Obedience to Christ

Who are we to please? 1 Thessalonians 4:1; Romans 15:1-2

God

Why? Romans 15:3

Christ Didn't Please Himself

How do believers have victory over Satan?

Ephesians 6:13	**Resist, Stand Firm in the Faith and Be Obedient to the Bible**
Ephesians 6:16	**Faith**
Ephesians 6:17	**The Sword of the Spirit, Which Is the Word of God**

How are believers to influence their world for Christ? Ephesians 5:10-12

A. **Learn What Pleases God**

B. **Reprove Evil**

Do you know that the Holy Spirit will stay in our lives? Philippians 1:6; Ephesians 4:30

God Will Finish the Work He Has Completed in Us in the Day of Christ (Day of Redemption)

CHAPTER 22: THE RAPTURE OF THE CHURCH

LAST DAYS OF THE CHURCH

Describe the last days of the Church. 2 Timothy 3:1-7
> **Lawlessness, Self-gratification, Ungodliness**

How does the present time of Grace end? 1 Thessalonians 4:16-18; 1 Corinthians 15:51-53
> **The Lord Jesus Returns to Catch up Believers**

How fast does the Rapture happen? 1 Corinthians 15:52
> **In the Twinkling of an Eye**

What happens to living believers at the Rapture? 1 Thessalonians 4:17
> **They Are Caught Up**

What happens to the dead in Christ? 1 Thessalonians 4:16
> **Their Bodies Are Caught up First**

What sounds will be heard? 1 Thessalonians 4:16
> **A Shout and a Trumpet Sound**

How will believers be changed? Philippians 3:20-21
> **They Will Receive Their Glorious Heavenly Bodies**

What is the destination of the Church? Ephesians 1:3; 2:6; 3:10; 6:9; Colossians 1:5
> **The Heavenlies (Heavenly Places)**

What is another name given for the Church? Romans 11:25
> **Fullness of the Gentiles (We Are in the "Fullness of the Gentiles" Which Lasts until the Church, the Body of Christ Is Finished, Complete, Full)**

What is called the fullness of Christ? Ephesians 1:22-23
> **The Church, the Body of Christ**

LIFE APPLICATION

God determined and knows the future. Where does He already see believers? Ephesians 2:6
> **Seated with Christ in Heavenlies**

What will believers be doing there? 1 Corinthians 6:2-3
> **Judging over Men and Angels**

In the ages to come, what does God want to show believers? Ephesians 2:7
   His Kindness And Riches of His Grace

How can anticipating Christ's return change our lives? 1 John 3:2-3
   It Can Help Us Clean up Our Lives

What happens to the Body of Christ, the Church, after the Rapture? 2 Timothy 4:1
   It Is Judged

CHAPTER 23: THE JUDGMENT (BEMA) SEAT OF CHRIST FOR REWARDS FOR SAVED

What does Jesus say in John 3:18?
   Whoever Believes in Christ Will Not Be Judged

Is a believer ever judged (condemned)? Romans 8:1
   There is No Condemnation

To whom is 2 Corinthians addressed? 2 Corinthians 1:1
   Saints (Believers)

Is the believer ever condemned in judgment? Romans 8:1
   No Condemnation

Who appears before the Bema Seat? 2 Corinthians 5:10
   Believers

What is the purpose of the Judgment Seat of Christ? 1 Corinthians 3:12-14
   Rewards

Why is the Judgment Seat of Christ necessary? 1 Corinthians 4:4-5
   Motives for What We Have Done

Name the crowns of glory and why these crowns are given?

2 Timothy 4:8	**Crown of Righteousness-for Those Who Love His Appearing**
1 Thessalonians 2:19-20	**Crown of Exaltation-for Those Who Have Led Others to the Lord**
James 1:12	**Crown of Life-for Those Who Persevere under Trial**
1 Corinthians 9:24-25	**Crown for Self-control**
Revelation 2:10	**Crown of Life for Those Who Are Martyred for Christ**

LIFE APPLICATION

Read: Colossians 3:23-24. What work will be rewarded?
Anything Done for Christ

Who is at work in believers? Philippians 2:13
God

Who will ultimately get the glory for the good done in our lives? Ephesians 1:6,12,14
God

MYSTERIES (SECRETS) OF THE BIBLE

What are some of these mysteries?

Romans 11:25	**Mystery of Partial Hardening of Israel**
Ephesians 3:3-7	**Mystery of Jew and Gentile in One Body, the Church**
Colossians 1:27	**Mystery of the Indwelling Christ**
2 Thessalonians 2:7	**Mystery of Lawlessness**
1 Timothy 3:9	**Mystery of Faith**
Matthew 13:10-11	**Mysteries of the Kingdom**

In the context of rewards, what are believers to do? 1 Corinthians 4:1-2
Be Stewards of the Mysteries of the Bible

The knowledge of God's Word, the Bible, is not only for a select few but it is meant for everyone.
What does God want us to do? Colossians 1:10
A. Please the Lord in All Ways
B. Bear Fruit by Doing Good Works
C. Study the Bible

CHAPTER 24: THE GREAT TRIBULATION FOR ISRAEL FOLLOWS THE RAPTURE OF THE CHURCH

What are some of the names given to this Great Tribulation time?

Matthew 24:21	**Great Tribulation**
Jeremiah 30:7	**Jacob's Trouble**
2 Thessalonians 2:2; 2 Peter 3:10	**Day of the Lord**
Revelation 6:16-17	**Wrath of the Lamb**
Daniel 9:24-27	**Daniel's 70th Week**

How does Satan deceive those who are living on the earth? Revelation 13:14
He Performs Signs and Miracles

What does Satan do? 2 Thessalonians 2:4
    A. He Exalts Himself
    B. He Seats Himself in the Temple
    C. He Says He Is God

What does Satan do to the people who do not worship his image? Revelation 13:15
    He Kills Them

What gospel will be proclaimed during the Tribulation? Matthew 24:14
    Gospel of the Kingdom

Who else preached the same gospel?
    The Lord Jesus Christ

What prayer will Israel once again pray during this tribulation time? Matthew 6:10-13
    The Lord's Prayer

What happens to those who do not take the mark of the Antichrist? Revelation 7:14-15
    They Have a Place Before the Throne

Name two reasons why Israel must be faithful until death. Revelation 2:10; Matthew 24:13
    A. To Receive the Crown of Life
    B. The One Who Endures to the End Shall Be Saved

What will be given to those who overcome? Revelation 3:5
    A. A White Garment
    B. Their Name Will Not Be Erased from the Book of Life

What is one of the first things Antichrist will do? Daniel 9:27
    Makes a Covenant with Israel

What happens after 3-1/2 years?
    A. Daniel 9:27   **Antichrist Puts a Stop to the Animal Sacrifices**
    B. Daniel 11:31   **The Sanctuary Will Be Desecrated**
    C. Daniel 11:36   **Anti Christ Exalts Himself above Every God**

How does the Great Tribulation end? Matthew 24:30
    Christ Returns

CHAPTER 25: JESUS CHRIST'S SECOND COMING FOR ISRAEL TO THE MOUNT OF OLIVES

Name two things that Jesus Christ, the Messiah, does to unbelievers. Matthew 24:30,39
- **A. He Gathers Unbelievers**
- **B. He Takes Them Away into Judgment**

How does Israel respond? Matthew 24:30
They Will Mourn.

Describe Jesus Christ's appearance when He returns. Revelation 19:11-16
- **A. Riding on a White Horse**
- **B. His Eyes Are a Flame of Fire**
- **C. Wearing Many Crowns**
- **D. Speaks the Word of God**

What is Israel's response to Christ at His second coming?
Zechariah 12:10   **Mourn and Weep**
Romans 11:26   **All Israel Will Be Saved**

When Jesus Christ returns, what does He bring with Him? Revelation 22:12
His Reward

What happens after Jesus Christ's return? Revelation 19:19
There Is a War

What is the name of this war? Revelation 16:16
Armageddon

Where will the battle of Armageddon be fought? Zechariah 12:11
The Plain of Megiddo

After the battle of Armageddon, what will happen to Satan? Revelation 20:2-3
He Is Bound

How long is Satan imprisoned? Revelation 20:7
1,000 Years

CHAPTER 26: DAVIDIC KINGDOM ESTABLISHED TO FULFILL PROPHECIES MADE TO ISRAEL

After Satan is imprisoned, what does Jesus Christ do? Revelation 20:4
He Reigns

How long does Jesus Christ reign? Revelation 20:4
1000 Years

Who will rule with Christ? Revelation 20:4
Those Who Have Not Worshiped the Antichrist

What will Israel inherit? Matthew 25:34
The Kingdom on Earth

What is the extent of the Kingdom? Zechariah 14:9
Over the Whole Earth

What does God promise Israel? Ezekiel 39:28-29
    A.   **Israel Will Be in Their Own Land**
    B.   **God Will Not Hide His Face from Israel**
    C.   **The Holy Spirit Will Be Poured out on Israel**

What does God build for Israel? Ezekiel 40:5
Temple

Where will Christ dwell in the Kingdom? Ezekiel 43:7
He Will Live in the Temple

What will be the position of the temple? Isaiah 2:2
It Will Be Raised Above the Hills

Who cannot enter the Temple? Ezekiel 44:9
Gentiles

What again will be observed? Ezekiel 44:15
Animal Sacrifices

What will be the duties of the priests? Ezekiel 44:24
    A.   **To Judge**
    B.   **Keep the Law**

What days will Israel again observe? Ezekiel 44:24
Feasts and Sabbaths

At the end of the one-thousand years, what happens to Satan? Revelation 20:7
Satan Is Let out of the Pit and He Deceives the Nations

How does God judge Satan and the deceived nations? Revelation 20:8-9
Fire Comes Out of Heaven and Devours Them

What happens to Satan, the False Prophet, and the Beast? Revelation 20:10
> **God Throws Them into the Lake of Fire, Where They Are Tormented Forever and Ever**

CHAPTER 27: <u>WHITE</u> <u>THRONE</u> <u>JUDGMENT</u> <u>OF</u> <u>THE</u> <u>UNSAVED</u>

When does the White Throne Judgment occur? Revelation 20:10-11
> **After Satan, the Antichrist and the Beast Are Thrown into the Lake of Fire**

Who stands before the White Throne for judgment? Revelation 20:12
> **The Unsaved Dead, Great and Small**

How will unbelievers be judged? Revelation 20:12-13
> **Out of the Book of Life and the Other Books**

What happens when their names are not found in the Lamb's Book of Life? Revelation 20:15
> **They Are Thrown into the Lake of Fire**

What book records the names of believers in Christ? Philippians 4:1-3
> **The Book of Life**

What determines the amount of punishment the unsaved will receive in the lake of fire? Revelation 20:12
> **Through Deeds on Earth**

What is the second death? Revelation 21:8
> **The Lake of Fire**

CHAPTER 28: <u>NEW</u> <u>HEAVEN</u>, <u>NEW</u> <u>EARTH</u>, <u>AND</u> <u>THE</u> <u>NEW</u> <u>JERUSALEM</u>

What honor will Jesus Christ be given? Philippians 2:9-11
> **A. Exaltation**
> **B. Everyone Will Confess That Jesus Christ Is Lord**

Name two things that Christ conquered. Revelation 1:17-18
> **A. Death**
> **B. Hell**

What follows the White Throne Judgment? Ephesians 1:10
> **The Fullness of Times When Things Are Finalized**

What new things does God make? Revelation 21:1-2
     A. New Heaven
     B. New Earth
     C. New Jerusalem

How is the present earth destroyed? 2 Peter 3:10
     Fire

Describe the New Jerusalem.

Revelation 21:2	**A City**
Revelation 21:11	**Bright and Shining in Appearance**
Revelation 21:12	**12 Gates with the Names of the Sons of Israel On it**
Revelation 21:14	**Foundation Stones with the Names of the Apostles on Them**
Revelation 21:16	**1500 Miles Square**
Revelation 21:21	**Gates of Pearl, a Street of Gold**
Revelation 21:22	**No Temple, the Lord God Himself is the Temple**
Revelation 21:23	**The Glory of the Lord Illumines the City**
Revelation 21:24	**The Glory of the Lord Illumines the Earth**
Revelation 21:25	**There is No Night**
Revelation 22:2	**A River of Life, Tree Bearing 12 Kinds of Fruit**
Revelation 22:5	**No Light of the Sun**

Who will see God and Christ's face? Revelation 22:3-4; 14:1
     The 12 Tribes of the Sons of Israel

What mark will they have on their forehead? Revelation 22:4; 14:1
     God's Name on Their Foreheads

Who will not be allowed to enter the New Jerusalem? Revelation 21:27
     Those Who Are Not Written in the Book of Life

Printed in the United States
6085